TUR

WORDS

TURNING
WORDS

TRANSFORMATIVE
ENCOUNTERS WITH
BUDDHIST TEACHERS

HOZAN ALAN SENAUKE

FOREWORD BY SUSAN MOON

SHAMBHALA

Shambhala Publications, Inc.
2129 13th Street
Boulder, Colorado 80302
www.shambhala.com

Cover art: Paisan Changhirun/Shutterstock; Limolida Design Studio/ Shutterstock; solarbird/Shutterstock
Cover design: Daniel Urban-Brown
Interior design: Katrina Noble

9 8 7 6 5 4 3 2 1

First Edition
Printed in the United States of America

Shambhala Publications makes every effort to print on acid-free, recycled paper.
Shambhala Publications is distributed worldwide by Penguin Random House, Inc., and its subsidiaries.

LIBRARY OF CONGRESS CATALOGING-IN-PUBLICATION DATA
Names: Senauke, Hozan Alan, author.
Title: Turning words: transformative encounters with Buddhist teachers / Hozan Alan Senauke; foreword by Susan Moon.
Description: First edition. | Boulder, Colorado: Shambhala, [2023] | Includes bibliographical references.
Identifiers: LCCN 2022014977 | ISBN 9781645471318 (trade paperback)
Subjects: LCSH: Globalization—Religious aspects—Buddhism. | Buddhism—Social aspects. | Religious life—Buddhism. | Zen Buddhism—Doctrines.
Classification: LCC BQ4570.G56 S46 2023 | DDC 294.3—DC23/ ENG/20220609
LC record available at https://lccn.loc.gov/2022014977

To my beloved teachers:
Hakuryu Sojun Mel Weitsman
and Kosei Nyokai Laurie Schley Senauke

CONTENTS

FOREWORD

In *Turning Words*, Zen priest and teacher Hozan Alan Senauke brings us a few dozen short tales about encounters with people he has known, with turning words at the center. The people in these stories are his teachers, guides, family members, friends, and Zen brothers and sisters, and the book is a contemporary version of the classic Chinese koan collections so important in Zen literature.

The phrase "turning words" refers to the words at the core of an old Zen koan. They are words that cause you to pivot so that you see the universe from a different angle or that turn you in another direction than the way you were headed, sending you on a different path. I love the old koans (some more than others), but they can seem dusty with time or stubbornly mysterious. Alan's tales are friendlier to the reader than the Tang dynasty koans, and you can recognize yourself more easily in them because of the modern, familiar context. The turning words here don't always sound particularly Zen. They can be words like "Are you happy?" or "I will not abandon you." But like the traditional koans, these stories can open us when we open them. Each one contains a kernel, sometimes in the form of a punch line; and even when they are funny, they are serious.

I met Alan at Berkeley Zen Center (BZC) over thirty-five years ago. (In a formal Zen setting, I address him as Hozan, but here, because he's my old friend, I will call him Alan.) I had already been practicing at BZC for several years when Alan showed up for serious, wholehearted practice. He was hairy compared to now, maybe even a little scruffy, both face and head unshaved. I thought he was hip; he played the guitar and sang folk songs at informal sangha gatherings, bringing energy and smarts into our sangha. Now—presto chango!— he's the abbot of the Berkeley Zen Center, without a hair on his head (not counting whiskers). Apparently transformed, living proof of the teaching that there is no fixed self, he's still uniquely Alan, not to be mistaken with any other person, and these stories come to us from the Alan who keeps on being Alan.

The change was not rapid and there were no magic tricks involved. A long friendship in which you witness each other's life passages along the way is tender. It's moving to see a friend grow and change over the years. I knew Alan when he went to practice at Tassajara Zen Mountain Monastery, where he met his partner, Laurie (whom you'll also meet in the course of this book), got married, moved into BZC as a resident, and became a parent. We worked together for fifteen years at the Buddhist Peace Fellowship, he as the director and I as the editor of our journal, *Turning Wheel*. For six of those years, our office was a tiny room that we rented from the Berkeley Gray Panthers, and our desks were just a few feet apart. We could have counted each other's sneezes if we wanted to.

I went to Alan's old-time music performances at Ashkenaz in Berkeley. I rejoiced with him when his records were released, when he took the precepts, when he was ordained. I knew him when he retired from the Buddhist Peace Fellowship and started the Clear View Project, a nonprofit providing Buddhist-based resources for relief and social change. I knew him when he received dharma transmission, when our teacher Sojun Mel Weitsman died, and when he became abbot of BZC in the middle of the COVID-19 pandemic. I joined the crowd who Zoomed with joy to his Mountain Seat Ceremony.

Over our long dharma friendship, I saw Alan soften, steady, and reach out more and more fluently to others, his compassion readily expressed. I saw him become a Zen teacher, and of course he keeps on *becoming*, because there is no final product of Zen practice called "teacher." This book is a wonderful quilt of teachings he has been receiving from others along the way.

The turning words in this book come from many different directions. At home, Laurie, also a Zen teacher, shares with him her motto, "I will not abandon you." His dharma brother Ross Blum, who lives next door, remarks, "Not that again!" His teacher Sojun Mel Weitsman suggests, "Let things fall apart."

From the wider community, the late Bernie Glassman, cofounder of the Zen Peacemaker Order, comments, "That's just my opinion, man." David Chadwick, writer and Suzuki Roshi archivist, explains, "I just have low standards." The Chan teacher Venerable Sheng Yen says, "Regulate your life." Maha Ghosananda, the great Cambodian peace activist, tells him, "The most important thing is eating." I leave it to you to find out the context of these enigmatic statements in the following pages.

This book is not a memoir, but as we are invited into Alan's conversations with teachers and friends in his everyday life and from far away, we get a sense of the breadth of his community and of his readiness to connect. Each section is named for the person whose words or gestures made a difference, including one on "Alan Senauke." This section turns out to be a modest offering, in which he speaks of his learnings, not of his teachings. He relates several moving anecdotes about discoveries he made through personal adventures, misadventures, and mistakes—experiences that, though mostly devoid of words, led him to fresh understandings. At the opening of this section he writes, "I see myself as the still-maturing child of all those practitioners who have come before me—in the same way a musician or an artist consciously or not draws from the ocean of creativity that precedes them, and gradually becomes authentic."

In a particularly touching story in this section, Alan is riding in a cab from the Calcutta airport to his hotel, but the driver, with whom Alan has no common language, can't find the address. After a good deal of zigzagging about in the darkness, he stops his cab in the middle of the street, wordlessly ushers Alan out, puts his bags into a rickshaw that happens to be there, and drives away. Alan climbs on board, and the rickshaw man pulls him through the Calcutta night to his hotel. No words are spoken in this episode, but the teaching seems to be that when you're anxious because of being in an unfamiliar situation, then, if you see that you are not in evident danger, you have the chance to let go into not knowing, to appreciate things as they are, and to trust what unfolds.

Now, because of his responsibilities as abbot, Alan must stay at home more than he used to, but he travels in time. Some of the turning words in this book come to him from ancestors of the past, like Huineng, the Sixth Chinese Ancestor, who said, "Sentient beings of my mind are numberless, I vow to save them." Indeed, a thread that runs through the book is Alan's ongoing and unequivocal commitment to saving beings, within and without. I have been inspired by this commitment as I have witnessed it in Alan's life, and again as it shows up in this book. Furthermore, he lets me see that his ability to make this commitment is a work in progress, as it must be with any human. Alan is never preachy. Not teachy, either. He's the learner here, and this encourages me, because I'm learning too.

When I first knew Alan, he talked faster and louder than he does now. I'm not saying it was *too* fast or *too* loud. He had a lot of good things to say and I'm glad he said them. His posture is more invitational now: his interest in hearing what others have to say is evident, and his desire to respond to the suffering of others is clear.

As Alan relates these stories of the wide sangha of people who are the buddhas and bodhisattvas of his life, he reminds me that turning words are everywhere, and he encourages me to be quiet and receptive enough to receive them when they come.

—SUSAN MOON

INTRODUCTION

Reverend Master, please say a turning word for me
and free me from this wild fox body.

—from "Baizhang's Fox," case 2 of *The Gateless Gate*

THROUGHOUT THE LONG HISTORY of Zen Bud-
dhism, teachers have offered "turning words" to their students. Many of the koans rooted in Chinese collections like
The Gateless Gate, the *Blue Cliff Record*, the *Book of Equanim-
ity*, along with the recorded sayings of great masters, pivot on
turning words. Such words—live language—blow open the
doors of perception.

Turning words are not just pithy sayings in old books. They
may not even be words at all. The early morning call of crows
on the rooftop are turning words. As my late teacher Robert
Aitken Roshi wrote, "Let the cry of the gecko put an end to
birth and death." Words are actions and actions are words.
They can occur at any moment in our living Zen tradition,
traded between students and teachers. In the mid-1960s, when
he was first taking up Zen, Sojun Mel Weitsman, founder of

the Berkeley Zen Center, asked Shunryu Suzuki Roshi, "What is nirvana?" Suzuki responded, "Seeing one thing through to the end." And that is what Sojun Roshi continued to do for fifty-five years, until the last days of his life.

○ ○ ○

In his "Instructions to the Cook," the thirteenth-century master Eihei Dogen speaks of Zen practice as the way "to turn things while being turned by things." The world is always turning, unfolding. We are turned by turning words, like the ones I offer in this book. Then each of us is responsible to turn things—to harmonize the world.

Seen from another angle, we inhabit the universal stillness, like the depths of the ocean—still, dark, and fluid. But there is always motion, even in the darkest depths.

I find the essence of Zen practice to be receptivity, open-mindedness. In our zazen practice, the instruction we get is to allow our senses to receive what is coming in but not to engage our thinking mind in these perceptions, not stringing them together into stories that limit our free-ranging mind. Sojun Roshi would encourage us to be like a frog by the side of a pond. The frog's keen senses are wide open. When a fly darts by, then . . . *zup!* With the flick of a tongue, lunch has been served.

For me, these turning words are like the fly. If I am calm and receptive, then I can respond instantaneously and turning words provide nourishment. If I am lethargic and dull-witted, then I will most likely miss the point and miss my lunch.

So I say as much to myself as to you: Please be awake! Don't be fooled by anything!

o o o

Each of the following stories recounts words I have heard or an encounter with someone whose actions have turned me. Maybe it is more accurate to say I was there when things were said or done. My perception may have been immediate—though, in some cases, immediacy arose only on further reflection. These turning words were offered me by bodhisattvas as skillful means, *upaya*. Even if I don't necessarily get it right away, the impact of what was said and done has remained with me for all these years. New (old?) memories still rise from deep in mind. They still turn me.

Remember that these teachers are not saints. Even Saints aren't necessarily saints. Like all of us, their characters have cracks and crevices. In certain areas, each teacher may have a particular brilliance and insight. In other areas, they can be shortsighted, even mistaken. They can be imperfect, incomplete. I have sidestepped critique here; others can speak to that. I think of my teachers in terms expressed by Walt Whitman in Part 51 of "Song of Myself":

Do I contradict myself?
Very well then I contradict myself,
(I am large, I contain multitudes.)
I concentrate toward them that are nigh, I wait on the door-slab.

I hope my simple telling of events carries something essential through the doors of your mind. Thus have I heard.

TURNING
WORDS

ISAAC SENAUKE

Are You Happy?

ISAAC SENAUKE WAS MY FATHER, known as "Lish" from childhood. In Hebrew the name Isaac means "one who laughs or rejoices." He was an engineer by training but preferred to work with his hands. Not a Zen teacher or practitioner by any stretch of the imagination, he told me that if he had another go at life, he would just be a "grease monkey," up to his elbows in machinery. When I was a child, I watched him carefully, as children do. In small ways he was always helping those around him—being a friend, jumping in to help them fix their car or boat, creating a sense of ease around him. I never knew him to cultivate any kind of spirituality—not the secular Judaism of his birth or any other path. But he was comfortable in his skin, down to earth, at home on the water. I knew him to be a master sailor in all kinds of seas or weather.

Our relationship was difficult. I think that he was troubled about leaving four children when he divorced my mother in 1960. This was a survival move for him. I understand that.

I knew it even then. But it meant I lost a father's necessary presence. At the same time, as the sixties unfolded, my values, activities, and unkempt appearance were attuned to the times, which alarmed him.

In truth, it alarmed me as well. My interests—literary, political, musical, etc.—were compelling, and I had good friends—many of whom are still my friends. But I was dogged by depression and, as I have written elsewhere in this book, by the existential question of what I was here on earth to do.

It must have been the summer of 1972 when my father and his wife Adele spent several days in San Francisco. They were returning from a trip to the South Pacific, where they had visited remote areas in what would now be called "adventure travel." Well, they were in town. At the time, my first marriage had moved from couples counseling to separation strategies. Sadly, it seemed we were not destined to grow up together. We had decided to part ways, but this was not something we wanted to share with my father. I dreaded getting into a discussion about it with him So, we pretended that everything was fine in our marriage, hoping he would buy the act. I don't think we were very good at it.

Here I come to the turning words. One afternoon during his visit, my father and I—just the two of us—were driving north from Palo Alto, where he had been visiting some old friends. He was driving and I was taking in the view. He turned to me and asked, "I want to know, are you happy?" This was one of those impossible questions. It stung me because, first, I had no answer, and second, the answer was "no." I don't remember my exact response, but it was something to the effect that happiness was not my standard or goal in life. "Being happy is not important to me. I want to be of use. That is how I want to live."

But his question has lingered for the last fifty years: "Are you happy?" The impact of my father's words were not sudden. The turning came very slowly, until I understood that we were both right. The point is to find happiness in the act of serving others. If joy or happiness is absent, then being of use is marked with a kind grim determination. If utility is missing from happiness, then it is easy to fall into a kind of soft-focus narcissism. Fortunately, he let me figure this out for myself. Actually, I am not sure he could have articulated how this all fit together. But I am grateful for the leading question.

Many of the teachers I have encountered, including the ones in these pages, bring a lightness of spirit to the work of saving sentient beings. Their joy and ease enlighten and enliven those who meet them. They take their work seriously, but they don't take themselves seriously. So, as they go through the world, there are no barriers to their happiness. They laugh a lot.

SOJUN MEL WEITSMAN

Going to the Root

IN THE ZEN TRADITION we say that the dharma is transmitted from "warm hand to warm hand." With one's own hand, one receives the essence of buddhas' and ancestors' practice from one's "root teacher." Just as Shunryu Suzuki Roshi was Sojun Mel Weitsman's root teacher, Sojun Roshi is my root teacher. It is surprising to reflect on how traditional my training path has been: practicing with Sojun day by day for nearly thirty-seven years; receiving from him lay ordination, priest ordination, and dharma transmission; feeling the permission to enter his study freely. Going to the root, or more truly, growing from the root.

I began working on these stories shortly after Sojun Roshi was diagnosed with cancer in the fall of 2019. The cancer advanced so slowly, and Sojun tolerated his treatments so well, that one could forget the sword hanging above his head. But it was always there, and in certain light the sword's shadow was stark and clear. Toward the later months of 2020, the cancer was taking its toll, and our dear teacher weakened. He died peacefully at home in early January 2021.

Even now, when I have become the second abbot of Berkeley Zen Center, I listen for the sound of his office door closing, his footsteps on our backstairs, or the sound of his voice—encouraging or chiding. I search the shifting sands of memory for Sojun's turning words, much the way he constantly shared Suzuki Roshi's words with us. This is how our teachers continue to live across time and space.

WHAT A ZEN TEACHER ISN'T

When I arrived at Berkeley Zen Center in the autumn of 1984, Sojun—or Mel as we familiarly called him—was in Japan receiving dharma transmission from Hoitsu Suzuki, Shunryu Suzuki Roshi's son. So just then there was no teacher around and BZC didn't yet have any other priests. But the community was well established.

For about a month, no one directly led our daily sitting and service, but there were long-term practitioners in residence and in the wider community—Maylie Scott, Fran Tribe, Ron Nestor, and others—whom I saw as role models. I watched them and asked a lot of questions. Most of all, I threw myself into zazen, which was never easy. Sitting was painful, unsettled, distracted, and boring. We sat forty-minute periods, and I was often sure that the bell ringer had fallen asleep at the wheel. But I persisted, and I still do, all these years later. There was something settled-seeming about people at BZC, and I hoped that I could become like them.

After a month, Mel returned from Japan as Sojun Sensei, wearing the brown robes signifying dharma transmission, affirming the maturity of his priestly practice and understanding. His quiet but confident manner helped bring my vision of Berkeley Zen Center into focus. I was grateful to find him a warm and modest man, devoid of self-promotion and the snares of charisma. Sojun was a steady presence at almost every period of zazen. I saw that his presence was the pivot around which our community turned.

On his return, Sojun put up a *dokusan* schedule with slots for private interviews. I knew this was an essential element of Zen training, although no one explained to me what happened in the interview room. Nevertheless, I signed up and my time arrived. BZC has a dokusan hut in the rear of our property. It is an intimate face-to-face tatami room, teahouse size, about seven by nine feet.

There was no instruction about what to say or ask in dokusan. But, like everyone else, I found my way. At first I was focused on physical pain—aching legs, that sticking pain in my shoulders, my inability to find a stable posture for my thirty-five-year-old body. These were my problems and everyone's problems. Sojun was very familiar with such matters because he had to work his way through each problem in his own practice. My questions extended to my own existential crisis: What was I doing on the planet? What might I make of my life? These, too, were the quotidian matters of Zen. Sojun's answers were rarely direct and never explanatory. He would often turn the language around and give it back to the student to figure out. I wanted something more and never got it.

After a time, I came to understand that Sojun was not my father, or my friend, or my psychotherapist. Each time I tried to place him in one of those boxes, he slipped away. He was my Zen teacher, a class of person I had not previously met in life. As a Zen teacher, his job was to be a mirror so I could see and free myself.

LET THINGS FALL APART

Long ago, in a chilly morning dokusan, Sojun gave me a sudden teaching: *Let things fall apart.*

This was a year or so into my practice. Life was unsettled in my midthirties, but after a decade wandering in the existential wilderness, I had found a home at BZC. Having a Zen teacher was a new experience. Sojun was disarmingly warm—despite the heat he could convey with a backward glance or the insistent tapping of a foot if, during service, your beat dragged on the *mokugyo* (a fish-shaped wooden drum). Some Zen teachers keep students on a short leash. Sojun's style was to encourage and watch, in accord with Suzuki Roshi's advice in *Zen Mind, Beginner's Mind*: "To give your sheep or cow a large, spacious meadow is the way to control him. So it is with people; first let them do what they want, and watch them."

I was surprised to find that I loved the Zen forms and found an affinity for them even though previous religious training suggested otherwise. Five years at the orthodox Great Neck Synagogue had not kindled even a spark of religious devotion. Hebrew lessons were dry as dust, and our chaotic and highly secular home included no Jewish religious practice at all. After the empty milestone of bar mitzvah in 1960, I never returned to the temple.

I thought I had disdain for ritual, but after years as a performing musician, I was a quick study at the forms of Zen: walking, bowing, formal eating practice, the intricacies of ceremonies including zazen itself. I could see how things in the zendo worked together: the flow of time and space. I watched Sojun carefully and saw his naturalness. He was very much in his body, while I was not. There was nothing inflated or egocentric in the way he moved in the world. In and out of the zendo, he seemed to walk right down the middle way—not offhanded, never stiff, but flexible.

At the same time, an ungainly creature appeared from the depths of my personality. It must have been lurking there, waiting for conditions to give it life. This creature was a perfectionist; he was judgmental, bossy, impatient, and highly verbal. He thought he was smarter than others and suffered because of that thought. As I learned more about the various jobs and positions others held at the center, I was critical of how they performed. I found myself getting into others' business. In a sense, this was simply mistrust manifest, unconsciously thinking I could do things better. On a psychological level, I feared loss of control. If I could not "fix" the situation at hand, I would be hurled into the void, lost. As a child I had a recurring dream: clinging to a speeding car or train, flung into space as it rounded a turn. Every time I had this dream, I awoke with a start before landing.

In time I got the message from some people that my critical tendencies pissed them off. I can't blame them. Meanwhile Sojun let me roam and ruminate, watching patiently. I like Suzuki Roshi's metaphor of a cow in a pasture, but at BZC I often felt like a bull in a china shop. Sojun sat unmoving, like a frog, watching me, not reacting. Then, one day, he pounced, swallowing me whole with a bottomless teaching: *let things fall apart.*

I understand that each of us must decide when to let things fall apart and when to work as hard as we can to ensure survival and allow for new things to arise. Letting things fall apart too easily leans toward resignation and laziness. That's not what Sojun had in mind. And trying to hold on to the present moment or circumstance is simply impossible. Nobody hands out an instruction book. This teaching was given to me as medicine, to bring me into balance. Sojun might very well tell another person in another circumstance the opposite.

I think of something else Suzuki Roshi said: "The most important point is to accept yourself and stand on your two feet." This is where I try to live. To simply let go and be myself, moment by moment. Fall apart and come together. Come together and fall apart.

KNOWING MY TRUE TEACHER

As I mentioned, Sojun gave his students a wide field, which allowed us to explore the variety of Buddhist practices. Most teachers tend to keep their students close. This intimate teacher-student relationship is very often seen as the heart of Zen training. Sojun himself was given this wide field by Suzuki Roshi, who asked him to cross the bay to set up a practice center in Berkeley. After Suzuki Roshi's death in December 1971, Sojun was very much left to figure out his own path and his own vision for a growing sangha in Berkeley. While he looked to other elders and to his community for guidance, Sojun's root teacher—alive or dead—has always been Shunryu Suzuki.

I felt that the counterpart to the freedom that Sojun gave me was accountability. Before I would go to practice or meet with another teacher, I went to Sojun, explained what I wished to do, and sought his permission. I remember only one occasion in which he hesitated. Aitken Roshi had encouraged me to study koans with one of his disciples who taught in the Bay Area. This was someone Sojun didn't know personally, so he expressed doubt. The next morning, he told me to go ahead. He told me that he hadn't had such opportunities and he thought I should explore the dharma.

Even though I was accountable to Sojun, I realized later that he took a risk when he allowed so much freedom to a student. My dharmic adventures were a little like being in an open marriage. Theoretically, everything is honest and aboveboard, but there is always the chance that you might fall in love. A student might be charmed by the romantic pull of a new teacher. It happens regularly. I can now see that I was sometimes infatuated with another teacher: their brilliance, their power, their words, their eyes. But there came a moment when it was clear to me who was and would continue to be my true teacher. From that realization, I have not wavered.

Aitken Roshi spent his eightieth birthday at San Francisco Zen Center. There was a celebratory dinner, then a simple ceremony in the zendo, which included a *mondo*, a ritualized public exchange between students and teacher, often styled as *hossen*, or dharma combat. A student approached Aitken Roshi in his teacher's seat and asked him, "What is your most satisfying moment as a teacher?" Aitken answered quickly: "When my student comes into the interview room and I see in her eyes that she's got it!"

The next morning, I had arranged a dialogue between Aitken Roshi and Sojun Roshi—Aitken Roshi called this a *zadankai*, an informal group exchange of ideas. Aside from the two of them, only four or five people were present, including me and Joan Sutherland as interlocutors. I asked Sojun the same question that had been presented to Aitken the night before: "What is your most satisfying moment as a teacher?"

Sojun was also quick to respond. "When my student changes her life."

These were turning words. In that moment, all question and doubt disappeared about who my true teacher was. What I heard Sojun saying, with no disrespect for Aitken Roshi, was that enlightenment was not a mental state or something that shone in one's eyes. What matters is how one lives one's life. Do we live for the liberation and betterment of other beings, sentient or insentient, or for self-improvement and enhancement of our own understanding? That clarity has never left me.

ALIGNMENT

Day after day at Berkeley Zen Center I watched Sojun Roshi enter the zendo in the half-light of early morning. He approached the altar slowly and paused to take in the array before him—the Buddha, Prajnaparamita, candles, flowers, incense bowls, small bodhisattva figures, and memorial cards for the recently deceased. With a slow, sure touch, Sojun set all these figures and objects in what he felt to be the proper alignment. To his painterly eye, each thing on the altar should occupy its own space in balance with everything else. Daily, he was showing how we can create harmony and alignment in our mind and life.

Shunryu Suzuki Roshi wrote, "The reason everything looks beautiful is because it is out of balance, but its background is always in perfect harmony." Sojun was acutely aware of the actuality and beauty of things falling out of balance. I felt that he was constantly demonstrating how to create a background of harmony, of alignment. Not just in rearranging the altar but in how to align our body in zazen—to sit like a buddha—and how to live in a way that is aligned with causes and conditions. Any time I enter the zendo, the conditions of my daily life may be out of balance, but the altar and the room itself—the background—are in harmony. And over the years, I've learned how to approach the altar with my own eye of balance. This is how I wish to live.

HAI

When you knocked on Sojun Roshi's door, if he was there—which you could tell by whether his blinds were open—he would answer, "*Hai!*" This translates from the Japanese as "yes," but it means more, something like "I hear you."

Sojun explained to me once that he had made a practice for himself of responding to each person who knocked. No matter what he was doing—reading, writing, calligraphy—he would set down his task and attend to the person in front of him. Sometimes you might feel his full attention was not quite there, but mostly it was. I always admired this practice and, unevenly, aspire to it myself.

Recently I have been reading the Hebrew Bible and have come across the word *hineni*. When God calls to Abraham, to Moses from the burning bush, to the prophet Isaiah, in each case these elders respond, *"Hineni"*—"Here I am." Again, in a deeper sense, it suggests a readiness to respond to whatever one is called to do. So I hear *hai* and *hineni* as parallel expressions of willingness and receptivity. Really this is the heart of zazen—a mind and body open to the call of each moment.

DON'T TREAT ANYTHING LIKE AN OBJECT

Years ago, before my days of Zen practice, I experimented with psychedelic substances. My friends and I saw them as experiments, as explorations in consciousness. Like others my age, I could tell many stories of these adventures—some funny, some weird, some frightening. But having discovered that there were more aspects of reality than I had previously seen, I wanted a wider and deeper view. This led directly to Zen practice, which fortunately was very different from the wild perceptions of LSD.

But there was a lesson common to zazen and the psychedelic experience. This boils down to something Sojun

Roshi said succinctly in a lecture: "Don't treat anything like an object."

In the middle of a psychedelic trip often one's self dissolves and that "I" becomes part of an undifferentiated, interconnected oneness. Sojun pointed to that oneness—where zazen expresses a reality in which there is no longer subject and object. That oneness, however, is not a oneness of flashing lights and sensorial marvels but a deep and ordinary oneness. Every thing and every being is part of me and I am part of it. Separation is an illusion.

Yet our perception of oneness still includes differentiation. Each person is unique. Each thing is a unique expression of causes and conditions that momentarily arise, fall away, and become something else, in an unending stream of dynamic activity. Marvelous. Mysterious.

SOJUN WEEPS

On the occasion of a Saturday lecture at BZC some years ago, Sojun Roshi took his seat and read a piece from Nyogen Senzaki's 1919 collection *101 Zen Stories*, which was republished in Paul Reps's classic *Zen Flesh, Zen Bones*. This is the story Sojun read.

THE TUNNEL

Zenkai, the son of a samurai, journeyed to Edo and there became the retainer of a high official. He fell in love with the official's wife and was discovered. In self-defense, he slew the official. Then he ran away with the wife.

Both of them later became thieves. But the woman was so greedy that Zenkai grew disgusted. Finally, leaving her, he journeyed far away to the province of Buzen, where he became a wandering mendicant.

To atone for his past, Zenkai resolved to accomplish some good deed in his lifetime. Knowing of a dangerous road over a cliff that had caused the death and injury of many persons, he resolved to cut a tunnel through the mountains there.

Begging food in the daytime, Zenkai worked at night digging his tunnel. When thirty years had gone by, the tunnel was 2,280 feet long, 20 feet high, and 30 feet wide.

Two years before the work was completed, the son of the official he had slain, who was a skillful swordsman, found Zenkai out and came to kill him in revenge.

"I will give you my life willingly," said Zenkai. "Only let me finish this work. On the day it is completed then you may kill me."

So the son awaited the day. Several months passed and Zenkai kept on digging. The son grew tired of doing nothing and began to help with the digging. After he had helped for more than a year, he came to admire Zenkai's strong will and character.

At last the tunnel was completed and the people could use it and travel in safety. "Now cut off my head," said Zenkai. "My work is done."

"How can I cut off my own teacher's head?" asked the younger man with tears in his eyes.

Reading this story, Sojun's voice cracked near the end. He paused to weep. This was very unusual. As I write these words, my eyes fill with tears. Why was Sojun weeping? Why am I weeping?

IMPERMANENCE

In the midst of the COVID-19 pandemic, we suspended our daily practice together in the spirit of "sheltering in place" and moved our long-established practice to a digital platform, which was new and unfamiliar. Let things fall apart.

One day, before the pandemic, during Saturday lecture, Sojun paused and looked around the zendo, taking in the graceful form of the place and the attentive faces ready to absorb his teaching. He talked about how much he appreciated the beauty of our zendo and the steadiness of our fifty-year practice. How solid it all appeared. "And yet," he said, "it could all disappear in a moment. *Pffftt . . .*" He waved his hand dismissively. Some smiled knowingly. Of course, that is the Buddha's teaching of impermanence. We all know that. But we didn't know and could never have imagined the way things are right now.

OUR LAST CONVERSATION

Shortly before he took to the hospital bed set up in the living room for the last two weeks of his life, I visited with Sojun early one afternoon. He was tired after lunch and meeting with another disciple wrestling with anticipatory grief. Sojun motioned me toward his easy chair in the front parlor and, with difficulty, wheeled his walker over there.

Reclaiming his breath and composure, he looked at me intently and said, "What's going to happen to all my stuff?" Although it was out of character for Sojun to explore his feelings openly, I realized that I could take this question on two levels. I thought about all the robes, books, calligraphy tools, artwork, and ritual objects that filled his office at BZC. I thought about the stuff of his mind and body: What happens when we die? I was moved by the intimacy of this question, irrespective of its meaning. I had no answer.

I don't know what happens when we die, but surely we don't bring any of our stuff with us. Oh, maybe we carry our karma. Sojun was clear over the years that he didn't know. Buddhist doctrine proposes a lot of complicated theories about karma and rebirth. When asked about death and rebirth, Sojun often said, "I don't remember." Now he would have another opportunity to find out, but, alas, then he would not be likely to tell us about it.

As for the material residue of ninety-one years, I said it would be helpful if he told me what he might want left to whom. He had no energy to deal with such things. This was hardly the main thing on his mind. So I said: "I'll do my best to make sure anyone who wants something to remember you by will have that opportunity." I thought of all the precious things he had worn or carried or handled and realized there was nothing beyond this conversation, this moment, that I wished to have.

THE WHITE DRAGON'S RELICS
on the first anniversary of Sojun's death
Like Jianyuan of the Great Tang
I foolishly search for relics of our late master
In ashes and dreams
Knowing they are not hidden there
Such relics can't be found
In billowing waves and scudding clouds
But in my heart and mind
Where *sarira* pearls are plentiful
When my eyes are open
These relics—words and deeds—
Shine like dragon's teeth
Lying on the bare ground of zazen
Where any of us may pick them up
With upright posture and a free mind
Now I become such a relic

HOZAN ALAN SENAUKE, JANUARY 7, 2022

JOANNA MACY

Despair and Empowerment

JOANNA MACY WAS ONE of the early leaders of Buddhist Peace Fellowship in the late 1970s. Coming to Zen practice in the mid-1980s, I was influenced by Joanna's first book, *Despair and Personal Power in the Nuclear Age,* where she articulated the radical perspective of "despair and empowerment" work. That writing evolved into Joanna's remarkable teaching and training, which I was fortunate to encounter when I started working at BPF in 1991.

I was familiar with my own despair for our society and for the perilous fate of our planet —the various species that inhabit it and the land, sea, and air itself. But Joanna was saying that despair emerges from compassion. When turned— in relationship with other people and beings—despair can return us to a wider circle of compassion, which we feel as empowerment. This is at the heart of Joanna's current teachings on "The Work That Reconnects."

Over the past thirty years, Joanna Macy has become a mentor and friend. Living near each other in Berkeley, we meet for lunch, sharing our lives and the concerns we have for the world. The transformational training she has offered around the world continuously evolves. It uses different names in different places: Despair and Empowerment, Deep Ecology. Active Hope, the Work that Reconnects. But each approach shares the same experiential vision. Joanna writes of the work as following

> a spiral sequence flowing through four stages beginning with gratitude, then, honoring our pain for the world, seeing with fresh eyes, and finally, going forth . . .
>
> The critical passage or hinge of the workshop happens when, instead of privatizing, repressing and pathologizing our pain for the world (be it fear, grief, outrage or despair), we honor it. We learn to re-frame it as suffering-with or compassion. This brings us back to life.[1]

Joanna's image of the spiral, turning and rising, was a turning for me. As was the example of her ceaseless efforts for the planet. Even in her nineties, Joanna's energy is strong and her vision clear.

But today's times are perilous, and hope can be hard to find. Joanna and I have frequently discussed this, and—of course—people ask her about it all the time. Joanna writes:

> In all great adventures there comes a time when the little band of heroes feels totally outnumbered and bleak, like Frodo in *The Lord of the Rings* or Pilgrim in *Pilgrim's Progress*. You learn to say "It looks bleak. Big deal, it looks bleak."[2]

We talked about this, and she expands on the metaphor, explaining that Frodo's task was simply to carry the Ring to Mount Doom. That was his job, impossible when you think about it. But Joanna answers the challenge—Frodo's and our own—"We just have a job to do. Don't waste my time."

DAVID CHADWICK

Low Standards

DAVID CHADWICK BEGAN to study with Shunryu Suzuki Roshi in 1965 and was ordained by him in 1971. In subsequent years, David wrote *Crooked Cucumber*, the definitive biography of Suzuki Roshi. He also created www.cuke .com—a sprawling "archival site on the life and world of Shunryu Suzuki and those who knew him." These turning words from David come to me secondhand from Laurie Senauke, so one might say, "Thus was I told."

In 1983, a scandal involving sex and misuse of authority brought the resignation of abbot Richard Baker and a pervasive atmosphere of discouragement and disorder to San Francisco Zen Center, which was then one of the largest and best-known Buddhist institutions in the West. While SFZC was trying to reestablish its balance, Laurie and David both served on its board. Often the meetings were stormy and chaotic.

After one meeting, Laurie observed that David appeared calm throughout the turmoil. She asked him how he had remained so calm when everything seemed about to fly apart.

David answered, "I just have very low standards."

CHÖGYAM TRUNGPA

Is This Buddhism?

FROM DARK CORNERS of our mind invisible influ-
ences speak turning words. My first encounter with Zen
practice was in Berkeley, in the summer of 1968, a time of
demonstrations, curfew, and swaggering police patrols in
the streets. My friends and I returned to New York City in
the fall, with every intention of continuing to practice, but
school, the war in Vietnam, and rattling uncertainty about
the future deflected me from the path of practice. It was fifteen years later that I resumed the path, then with unswerv-
ing determination.

   In 1970, the Tibetan Buddhist master Chögyam
Trungpa, holder of both Kagyu and Nyingma lineages,
arrived in the United States and began to teach. His
method was deeply unorthodox, remarkably adaptive, and
alarmingly transgressive. America had never seen his like.
Nor has it since. An old friend of mine became Trungpa's
student on first encounter in Boston and was part of the

community that formed around him at Tail of the Tiger in Barnet, Vermont (later called Karmê Chöling), and then at the Naropa Institute in Boulder, Colorado. In time, several other friends of mine became Trungpa's followers, and this included former students of Suzuki Roshi after he died in 1971. Suzuki Roshi and Trungpa Rinpoche were very close from their first encounter at Tassajara.

I never saw or heard Trungpa in person. And it wasn't until later that I encountered his remarkable writing in books such as *Cutting Through Spiritual Materialism*, *Meditation in Action*, and *The Myth of Freedom*. But I heard stories that drifted through the spiritually inclined counterculture. Stories of endemic drunkenness, drug use, and rampant sexuality involving students and teacher alike. Details were scarce, but I didn't disbelieve the stories. I imagined my friends in such settings, and questions arose: "Is this Buddhism?" And, "What is Buddhism?"

These questions stayed in the back of my mind for twenty years, in tension with images of disciplined, upright, black-robed Zen monks. Although Zen has its own crazy wisdom tradition, that tradition seemed to reside in the record of ancient masters. Trungpa's actual or seeming transgressions, and those of his students—my peers—were here and now. This was a living tension, a creative tension—wild freedom and contained awareness—that lightly fanned the ember of bodhicitta within me for all those years, until it flamed up. So, without ever having met him, I respect and bow to Chögyam Trungpa among my teachers—for his dharma, not for his actions. Can one make such a distinction? That's a whole other question. But for all our sake and his, it saddens me that he was gone so young.

DAININ KATAGIRI

Karma and Rebirth

TWO STORIES ABOUT Dainin Katagiri Roshi.

In 1963, Katagiri came to the United States to serve Soto Zen communities in Los Angeles and San Francisco. From 1969 to 1971 he helped Suzuki Roshi build San Francisco Zen Center and Tassajara Zen Monastery. After Suzuki's death, Katagiri Roshi moved to Minneapolis, where he established the Minnesota Zen Meditation Center. In 1984, following the resignation of Richard Baker as abbot of SFZC, Katagiri Roshi was invited back to San Francisco to serve as interim abbot. It was at that time that I had a chance to practice with him, then to continue that practice at MZMC and at its rural practice center of Hokyoji.

The first of these stories does not really qualify as "turning words."

During lecture in *sesshin* at Hokyoji, Katagiri said that the next day he would explain karma and rebirth to us, because people were always asking about this in *dokusan*. There was general excitement. The Zen master was going to give us the lowdown on matters that most of us found perplexing, even irrational, or at least not subject to reasonable analysis. The next day arrived and Katagiri Roshi sat down to lecture. He was silent for a few moments and then spoke. "Karma is volitional action, which always has a fruit or a result . . ." Then he was silent before beginning again. "Rebirth is . . . rebirth means . . ." More silence, while he sat there with a look of perplexity on his face. At last, he said, "I'm sorry. I cannot talk about this or explain it to you. The problem is, I believe, and you do not." And that was that.

APPROACHING EMPTINESS

I have wonderful sense memories of sitting at Hokyoji. The summer air was thick. At night the howls of coyotes and timber wolves carried across the hills just west of the Mississippi. The zendo itself was a temporary structure, with a canvas roof tied down like a tent. When the wind rose, it blew across the roof and the stays; the sound was like the wind at sea filling the sails, whistling and creaking through the rigging. The only thing missing was a swaying hull cutting the waves.

The zendo was otherwise silent. After several days the energy of concentration was very strong. Meditating in the waning light of evening, I felt the grasp of what I thought of as "myself" was slipping away. It was like dropping into a warm, deep darkness. This dropping away, which Dogen writes of as the heart of Zen ("Drop body and mind") itself evoked primal fear—nothingness, death. By coincidence, Katagiri Roshi touched on this kind of experience the following day. The message I remember was that there was nothing to be afraid of. Let the self go and fall back into the arms of Buddha.

That night, as the wind came up and I merged with the sound of canvas and rope, I trusted Katagiri Roshi's words and allowed myself to merge with the world that could not be seen as inside or outside of me. Just breathing, being breathed, listening, falling back into the arms of Buddha for a few precious moments remembered all these years later.

HOZAN ALAN SENAUKE

What Is My Teaching?

IS IT PRESUMPTUOUS to include myself with these teachers who have been so instructive to many of us? Maybe so. But I can always make a mistake on purpose. As I reflect on all of these memories, it is difficult to see myself. Or . . . I see myself as the still-maturing child of all those practitioners who have come before me—in the same way a musician or an artist consciously or not draws from the ocean of creativity that precedes them and gradually becomes authentic.

What I tend to teach, the stories I tell, naturally draw from the teachers on these pages and the turning words I've gleaned from them. The challenge is to reveal or share what I authentically know, not just what I have read, heard, or seen. To quote Shunryu Suzuki Roshi, "The most important thing is to accept yourself and stand on your own two feet." But I know that buddhas and ancestors are always standing behind me.

COMING HOME

At some point in 1984, at the age of thirty-six, I felt I had run out of the script for my life. I left the band I had moved out west to join—Blue Flame Stringband. I had no regular job, no creative outlet, and no intimate relationship. I was fortunate, however, to have an excellent psychotherapist in Berkeley—Jane Ariel. One day I brought a pressing existential question to our therapy session, basically asking, "What is my purpose on this planet?"

Jane said, "That's an important question, but it's not a psychotherapeutic question. It's really a spiritual matter. You might want to look in that direction."

Oh . . . I thought about Zen, which I had briefly taken up in the summer of 1968. So I read a few Zen books and decided to visit Berkeley Zen Center, where I had practiced all those years ago. Back then, BZC was in a beautiful old house on Dwight Way, with a huge palm tree out front and a lovingly constructed zendo in the attic. The house was still there, but the Zen Center had moved a half mile to Russell Street.

I found the address and phone number and called for the sitting schedule. Someone I have never been able to identify answered the phone, and I explained that I had done some zazen years ago and hoped to pick up the practice again. His blunt and enigmatic response was this: "Find a blank wall, sit down, and stare at it." I couldn't believe this was the instruction I was getting on the phone. Clearly this was a place I had to check out.

Several evenings later I went for zazen instruction at BZC. Fran Tribe, who later became a close friend and mentor, was the zazen instructor. I began attending evening zazen at 5:40, sitting with the residents and other students from Berkeley, Oakland, Albany, and El Cerrito. I was home. I knew that immediately, without really understanding why. This was what I needed to be doing.

That continues to be my experience. I moved into BZC as a resident a year later, and I have been living there for more than thirty-seven years. Laurie and I got married and have been living there as a family since 1989. Our children Silvie and Alex were raised at Berkeley Zen Center and consider it home. It is home.

SESSHIN DESIRE

My first daylong sitting at Berkeley Zen Center must have been in January 1985. It was a long day with painful knees and intrusive thoughts. *When will this be over?* Throughout the course of the morning a persistent desire took shape. I kept thinking about a hamburger. Really! This desire just got stronger, even after a satisfying *oryoki*-style lunch in the zendo. After lunch, we had an hour-long break, and this imaginary hamburger could not be denied.

I had enough break time to go across Adeline Street to the Berkeley Bowl, our bountiful local market. I cruised the aisles envisioning this hamburger. In the bakery section, my eyes fell on a bagel—round, brown, about the same thickness as my imagined hamburger. I bought the bagel, the urgency for a hamburger disappeared, and I was satisfied.

This seems laughable, but, on reflection, the whole experience points to something deeper about the nature of (my) mind. I imagined a hamburger based on past desire and out of a wish to escape from my painful legs and mind, which were also part of my imagining mind. Because our imagination is so powerful, such an integral part of our way in the world, a bagel can serve in place of a hamburger. Our practice is to watch the mind. Endlessly fascinating.

SOMETHING IS MISSING

There is a passage from Dogen Zenji's *Genjokoan* that has long been a compass point for me.

> When dharma does not fill your whole body and mind, you think it is already sufficient. When dharma fills your body and mind, you understand that something is missing.[3]

What is missing? Essence, a fixed self, permanence, enlightenment—all those things we might decidedly wish for. The nature of our physical existence and mental perceptions shows us that things are always changing. Nothing is complete, except the true nature of *no thing*. As Shunryu Suzuki Roshi writes,

> I discovered that it is necessary, absolutely necessary, to believe in nothing . . . No matter what god or doctrine you believe in, if you become attached to it, your belief will be based more or less on a self-centered idea.[4]

If "something is missing," this means that everything we know or do is in some way incomplete. That has to be okay because that is precisely how it is. So, after Dogen's pronouncement: "When dharma fills your body and mind, you understand that something is missing," I would add a capping verse: "And that is just fine."

MUTUAL ACCOUNTABILITY

The teaching of Buddhist morality is our practice of the precepts, *sila* in the Pali language. Shodo Harada Roshi once said to me that if there were no people, there would be no precepts. At the heart of precept training is relationship—to others and, of course, to ourselves.

From this understanding and from the work I have done with my teachers and with students many years, I have arrived at the principle of mutual accountability. As a being in equality with all others, I am accountable to each of them for my words and actions. Likewise, they are accountable to me. While this may seem obvious in a social or political sense, it is radical in terms of our usual power dynamics.

Usually a student is accountable to the teacher. But usually is not always so. Sometimes the student is the student, and the teacher is the teacher. Sometimes the teacher is the student. And sometimes the student is the teacher. Student and teacher have a karmic connection, based on respect and honesty. They bow to each other.

Old buddha Joshu spoke about this as he left on pilgrimage at the age of fifty-seven. "Even a seven-year-old child, if he is greater than I am, I'll ask him to teach me. Even a hundred-year-old man, if I am greater than he is, I'll teach him." Joshu continued on the pilgrimage like this for twenty more years until he began to teach.

This is an explicit matter that I discuss with students. We give each other permission to say what we see in each other. If the student feels I have made a misstep, they can point this out and ask me about it. And I have a student's permission to inquire and comment on what I observe of their words and deeds. That is mutual accountability.

INTENTION AND IMPACT

Several years ago, I was teaching the Friday night open meditation at East Bay Meditation Center. EBMC is a remarkable place, dedicated to the inclusion of those often underrepresented or overlooked in so-called mainstream Buddhist communities in the United States.

My attention was drawn to the center's "Agreements for Multicultural Interactions" posted prominently by the side of the altar. The third agreement was a turning for me.

UNDERSTAND THE DIFFERENCE BETWEEN
INTENTION AND IMPACT
Try to understand and acknowledge impact. Denying the impact of something said by focusing on intent is often more destructive than the initial interaction.

In all my years of study and practice, intention has been a central principle. Right intention (*samma sankappa*) is the intention to awaken completely. In greater detail it includes the intention of renunciation, the intention of goodwill, and the intention of harmlessness. On the Eightfold Path, intention is the link between right view and right speech, between wisdom and moral activity. But an emphasis on "impact" recognizes that mundane intention is conditioned, and so its impact may be distant from what I intended. Hidden bias, cultural habits, and garden-variety ignorance can account for this difference. So I've been learning to pay attention to how my words and actions land on others, despite the best of intentions. This is how I practice relationship lately—or try to.

ON TOP OF THE WORLD

For fifteen years I made frequent trips to India to visit friends in Ambedkarite Buddhist communities. India, as you can imagine, is worlds away from the generally comfortable life in Berkeley. The streets are teeming with people and traffic. There are barriers of caste, religion, and multiple languages complex beyond my understanding and experience. A traveler like myself can readily feel lost at sea.

I parted company with a friend on arrival at the Kolkata airport. It was about 6:00 p.m. when I got my luggage and lined up for a taxi to the hotel I had booked. On the map, it was only twelve miles from the airport to Hotel Gulshan, close to the Maidan at the center of the city. But we started out in the madness of rush hour, and after two long, choking hours we still had not arrived at the hotel. I guess we were lost.

My driver, who spoke no English, appeared to understand the hotel address, but after wandering about for another half hour he gave up. He stopped at a busy street corner and removed my bags. I thought we had arrived, but no. Without speaking to me, he recruited a wiry man pulling a rickshaw by hand. They both gestured me onto a high seat, handed up my bags, and the cabdriver sped away.

We moved very slowly through streets full of evening shoppers. I felt myself a spectacle for curious Bengali eyes. Then there was the troubling moral issue of being pulled along by a man with a yoke across his shoulders and not an ounce of fat on his body. Meanwhile, where were we?

I was beset by the strangeness and discomfort of my situation. So far from my "normal" life. In a moment, however, these concerns—the suffering of habitual anxieties—dropped away. I was fine, in no danger at all. I had money in my pocket, and the night market was fascinating as we rode by. My breathing settled. I sat upright on the rickshaw and took it all in as we moved slowly through the streets.

In a short while, we stopped in front of a marble-faced building with a gilded sign reading Hotel Gulshan. We had arrived. Stepping out of the rickshaw, I paid the driver, then doubled his modest fee as a tip. I slept well that night, and in the morning took another taxi to the airport for my flight home to California.

HOZAN KUSHIKI

I had *jukai*, or lay ordination, at Berkeley Zen Center with Sojun Roshi in June 1987. In this ceremony, one receives the sixteen bodhisattva precepts, or ethical teachings. One also receives a lineage document, *kechimyaku*, tracing a "bloodline" from Shakyamuni Buddha through ninety-something generations of Indian, Chinese, Japanese, and American teachers, with one's new Buddhist name at the foot of the document.

The Buddhist name(s) Sojun gave me consists of four characters. My "way name" is *Hozan*, Dharma Mountain. A way name broadly indicates what a teacher sees as the visible dimension of one's practice or character, the part of an iceberg that rises above the ocean's surface. One's "dharma name"—the second set of two characters—is aspirational. It speaks to qualities that are present in the student but need to be brought forth in the spirit of realization.

My dharma name is *Kushiki*, two pivotal characters in the *Great Wisdom Beyond Wisdom Heart Sutra*, which we chant every day. *Ku* translates as "emptiness," "formlessness," "boundlessness." *Shiki* is "form" or "color." The Heart Sutra says, "Form is not separate from emptiness; emptiness is not separate from form."

Usually when one uses one's Buddhist name, the second, or dharma, name is the one to put forward. But I chose to use Hozan, because I was not comfortable thinking of myself as Mr. Formless Form. In the late nineties, we had several naming workshops where Western priests were instructed by senior Soto Zen priests from Japan in the principles of creating dharma names for our students. Kushiki, however, brought forth a mixed expression of confusion and consternation from our Japanese friends. Constructed, as it is, of these two pivotal and abstract principles—formlessness and form—it was just not a conventional name. But our friends were polite, out of respect for Sojun.

Why did he give me this unconventional name? Actually, we never spoke about it directly. My guess is that, at the time, he saw me as stuck on the formal aspects of Zen. Sojun was asking me to include everything in my zazen and in my life, to flow like water, taking whatever form is needed.

I still go by the name Hozan, which is more conventionally Buddhist. But I have taken Kushiki to heart. The name is my teacher's deep question. Can I manifest the form of Zen, moment by moment, without special rituals or clothes, using plain words? Can I embody formlessness, boundlessness, within the form of zazen, within my whole life? This work is never done.

MOURNING DOVES

Can't you hear those lonesome doves?
Cooo-wee—woo woo wooo
Yes, I hear them
Mourning doves
Calling to each other
One east, one west
One higher in pitch, one a little lower
Two moons in the mind's sky
While we sit at dawn
Morning light pierces the dark curtain
And these enchanting visitors speak
Sweet turning words
Right now—I am nothing but the doves' call

Cooo-wee—woo woo wooo
Lost in a moment outside of time

HOZAN ALAN SENAUKE, APRIL 2, 2022

TENSHIN REB ANDERSON

Meeting on the Path

THERE IS SOMETHING disarmingly intense about Reb Anderson. Anyone who has met him knows what I mean. He is soft-spoken, brilliantly discursive in thought, and fundamentally kind. He is also lean, muscular, and energetically compressed. Maybe, enough said. In private interviews and *dokusan*, it seems he sees right through you.

In January 1988, at the watershed age of forty, I joined the practice period led by Reb at Tassajara Zen Monastery, deep in California's coastal Ventana Wilderness. Zen monastic practice is deep and quiet and hard. New monks, in particular, are cornered by their own habits and patterns, their likes and dislikes. Each day is a seamless schedule of zazen, work, and liturgy. There is no time "for yourself"—forgetting that no one else but yourself decided to go to a monastery in the first place.

One of the sweet practices at Tassajara is to stop and bow to each person whose path one crosses on the temple grounds. This practice helps us slow down and acknowledge that we are doing Zen together. Early in my time there, on a chilly day, I was walking along between the stone dining room and the kitchen. Reb and his attendant were approaching from the other direction, engaged in conversation. I cannot remember quite what happened internally or externally. Reb and his attendant stopped to bow, but I recall that I was thrown off-center and didn't get around to my bow until we were all continuing on our way.

A few days later I met with Reb for dokusan and I was still thinking about my loss of composure. Reb was sympathetic. He offered this reflection.

"When Hoitsu (*Suzuki*) walks into a room, everyone starts to laugh. When Mel walks into a room, everyone goes, 'Hi, Mel.' When I (*Reb*) walk into a room, people think, 'What am I doing wrong?'" He explained that each of us responds to another's character and energy. That's the way we are. And yet it behooves us to look at these patterns of response and ask how we would like to be seen in the world.

WHAT IS A ZEN MASTER?

I met with Reb at Green Gulch Farm to work on plans for Sojun Mel Weitsman's long-delayed funeral. Sitting across the table from him, here was the same man I practiced under thirty-four years ago at Tassajara. Now, though he had reached the age of seventy-nine, I saw only subtle marks of age around his eyes. Face-to-face, Reb still has a kind of seamless quality—compact, like a coiled spring. His soft and measured voice hints at depth and intensity held in reserve.

After a productive planning session, we talked about our families, what our children were doing. I mentioned that during the pandemic, my son, Genpo, had spent a year and a half training with Shodo Harada Roshi in Japan. I asked if Reb had ever met Harada Roshi, an important teacher for me. Reb said that he had not met him but had encountered several of Harada's dharma brothers, who had all been students of the twentieth-century Rinzai master Yamada Mumon Roshi. He spoke of a meeting with Mumon Roshi, sharing with me a turning moment.

Mumon Roshi made two visits to Tassajara in the early 1970s, after Suzuki Roshi had died. Mumon Roshi was welcomed and appreciated by the students there. In the 1980s, while traveling in Japan, Reb stopped to see Mumon at his temple. Far from the sparkling and engaging master Reb had met at Tassajara, Mumon Roshi, now in his mid eighties, was frail and silent, seemingly distant from the world. His attendants and caretakers had carefully dressed the Roshi in formal robes and placed him in his seat. But he was truly not responsive. This was the teacher of whom Zen scholar Victor Hori wrote, "Outside the *sanzen* room, he looked and acted like a tiny, wispy, immaterial Taoist hermit, but . . . inside the *sanzen* room, he suddenly turned into a lion."[5]

At this meeting, the lion did not appear.

Sitting there at Mumon Roshi's temple in Kyoto, Reb thought, "What is a Zen master?" Such a live question! Is a Zen master a person who has awakened completely? Someone who has received a certain authorization? When that person's body or mind has declined, in a conventional or medical sense, is the master still present? Mind you, these are my questions, not Reb's conjecture. I did not ask him for explanations. For that matter, I have arrived at my own answer, but I'll keep it to myself. What is a Zen master? What do you think?

KOBUN CHINO OTOGAWA

Dharma Joy

BECAUSE I TOOK PART in the winter 1988 practice period at Tassajara, I was fortunate to be around Reb Anderson and Sojun Weitsman when they offered their first dharma transmissions, authorizing students as full Soto Zen priests. Much preparation went into translating the elaborate ceremonies, gathering the necessary equipment, preparing the ritual spaces, and finally enacting the weeklong process—all of which had to be done in relative secrecy, often in the middle of the night or very early in the morning, before the rest of the monastic community awoke.

Two of our respected Japanese teachers were invited to guide and assist: Hoitsu Suzuki Roshi, whom I had previously met, and Kobun Chino Roshi, whom I only knew from puzzling but intriguing stories of his iconoclastic ways. This was the moment when I could see for myself.

Kobun Chino Otogawa was invited to San Francisco from Japan by Suzuki Roshi in 1967 to serve as his assistant at Tassajara. Coming from a Soto temple family, Kobun had trained at Eiheiji for three years and studied with Kodo Sawaki Roshi, himself an iconoclastic and unconventional Zen master. After Suzuki Roshi's death in 1971, Kobun became the teacher at Haiku Zendo in Los Altos, as well as the founder of Jikoji in Los Gatos, California; Santa Cruz Center; and Hokoji, near Taos, New Mexico. Tragically, he drowned in Switzerland in 2002 while trying and failing to save his daughter Maya.

Kobun lectured one morning in the dining room. I have no recollection of what he spoke about, but two indelible memories remain from that morning. At several points during the talk there were long pauses in the middle of a sentence. When I looked up, I could see that Kobun's chin had dropped to his chest. A moment later he reset his posture and completed his sentence and thought. To this day Kobun Chino Roshi is the only teacher I have seen fall asleep at his own lecture.

When the talk was over, we stepped out into the courtyard. It was a crisp, clear winter morning. The morning colors were brilliant. The surrounding mountains shone green and gold. Everything felt alive. I was alive. Reb Anderson was standing next to me. I remarked on the vivid experience of Kobun's lecture and this moment we were both inhabiting. I asked, "What is this?"

Reb said, "Dharma joy."

WATCH

In Soto Zen monasteries it is customary to have a more relaxed schedule on calendar days ending in 4 and 9, with time for the monks to shave and bathe, do laundry, write letters, and get a little extra rest. During *ango*, or practice period, at Tassajara, there is often a special breakfast or dinner served family style in the dining room, rather than the usual *oryoki*-style meals in the zendo. Tassajara cooks go all out on these 4/9-day meals with gourmet vegetarian cooking and always a rich, sugary dessert.

At one such meal in the winter of 1988, I was fortunate to be sitting with Kobun Roshi and some of his family. I think that in those days, Kobun was generally following a macrobiotic diet, which, among other things, avoids refined sugars. The moment arrived for servers to bring out the dessert. Kobun turned to those of us at his end of the table, saying, "Watch. Watch what happens when they serve dessert." My memory may not be accurate, but I want to say they carried in platters of something like a Baked Alaska.

Before the Zen students had taken a mouthful, even before the dishes were set on our tables, the ambient sound in the room skyrocketed, an explosion of excited words.

Kobun Roshi looked around calmly, smiled, and said one word: "Sugar."

ZENGYU PAUL DISCOE

The Old Ladies of Sakamoto

IN THE SPRING of 1989, just three days after I was ordained as a novice Zen priest, Paul Discoe led a group of disorderly Zen students—all men in our thirties and forties—to spend a month at Suzuki Roshi's temple Rinso-in. We were an unruly, impatient bunch, and I now regret how hard we made things for Paul. But that's another story.

Rinso-in is an old and beautiful Soto Zen temple, built five hundred years ago. It sits up against a mountain with satsuma trees on the lower slopes. The heights are planted with renowned Shizuoka tea, rolling out for miles. Rinso-in is cared for by the Suzuki family. In those years the head priest was Hoitsu Suzuki Roshi, along with his wife, Chitose, and their young children.

Down a winding road from the temple is the crossroads village of Sakamoto, a few miles from Yaizu, a busy fishing port. We often wandered down to the small corner store in Sakamoto for snacks and last-minute groceries. Once we had settled in at Rinso-in for a few days, Paul spoke to us about how to understand what we were seeing day by day at the crossroads.

He told us to watch the old ladies who meet on the narrow bridge in town. Often their backs were bent from years of inadequate diet during the war and postwar years. But they had a lightness of motion and expression that was clear even from a distance. They would encounter each other, stop, exchange words, and bow continuously, bobbing up and down like those "drinking bird" toys. Paul explained that the words exchanged—on the order of "How are you?" "How is your family?" "Nice weather today," and such—were not significant. The essence of their connection was in how kindly and warmly they bowed to each other. Once I realized that, I have always marveled at the intimacy of Japanese culture, which can otherwise seem so layered in formality.

HOITSU SUZUKI

The Master Kicks a Tire

DURING THAT SPRING 1989 practice period in Japan, most of our month was spent at Rinso-in, where Suzuki Roshi's son Hoitsu Suzuki Roshi was the head priest. We first arrived at the temple after midnight, exhausted from a very long flight and the complete confusion of landing in Japan on the eve of Golden Week, when seemingly the whole country was on the move—mostly on the trains we needed to take.

Anyhow, walking into the *hondo* (the main hall) at Rinso-in, I saw a community alive with members preparing local crafts to sell the next day at a benefit for orphans in Cambodia. People were laughing, chatting, snacking, wrapping, and organizing pottery, floral arrangements, and other crafts. They welcomed us warmly, and I knew immediately that I was home. Silently I asked myself, *How can you know this?* But I was certain I was home. And this has proven to be true over all these years.

Our little group set up a three-week practice period at Rinso-in, a wonderful time. Toward the end of this time, Taizan Maezumi Roshi paid us a surprise visit. Hoitsu Roshi—whom we called Hojosan, or "Mr. Temple"—heard Maezumi Roshi's elegant white Honda sedan pull into the temple's gravel lot. Meanwhile, the rest of us had been relaxing in our *suryo*, the informal quarters—drinking tea, writing letters, folding laundry, dressed in general disarray. Hojosan ran in and started gathering up the cups and snacks, telling us to get dressed right away and get the laundry out of sight. Maezumi Roshi had arrived on an inspection tour. What were these Americans doing at Rinso-in?

I think we passed the inspection. With Hojosan, we all lined up in the temple courtyard and bowed to Maezumi Roshi and his priestly chauffeur as they drove away in their fancy car, over the small bridge, past the moss-covered arhats, down the hill to Sakamoto and Yaizu.

Hojosan's rusting orange Toyota was parked in the far corner of the courtyard. He walked over to the car and we followed. Tentatively, he kicked a tire and a bit of dirt fell from the fender. Hoitsu scratched his bare skull, shook his head in mock dismay, and walked away.

CHITOSE SUZUKI

Mottainai

SUZUKI OKUSAN, Hoitsu Roshi's lovely wife, was the only woman at Rinso-in spring 1989 when we had a practice period there. The Suzuki children were away at school and work, and we were the errant American children. I suppose we all had a crush on her, but Chitose Suzuki was and is independent and fierce. She did not fit the demur stereotype of a temple wife. This is an empty stereotype. Probably no Japanese woman fit this caricature of a temple wife, because they had to be tough to make an austere temple life work.

I was *tenzo* (head cook) for our month at Rinso-in, responsible for turning out three meals a day in a tiny kitchen with a two-burner gas stove and a big rice cooker. We had rice, in one form or another, two or three times a day. Rice porridge, sticky rice, brown rice when I could find it. For flavor I might add broth, onions, or chestnuts. But a lot of rice.

Often there was a crust of slightly scorched rice, *okoge*, on the bottom of the cooker, very tasty with *shoyu*, Japanese soy sauce. And when the lid was lifted off the cooker, there was a thin, transparent skin of starch resting on top of the rice.

Our humble cooking facility was right next to the Suzuki family's living quarters. Suzuki Okusan would frequently look in on us to see how we were doing. She paid particular attention to how we were cleaning up after the meal. She watched us clean the rice pot, scraping the scorched rice from the bottom and skimming the rice starch from the top. The cooks gobbled up the tasty okoge, and we consigned the skin of rice starch to the trash. Chitose's eagle eye caught this one morning. She shouted at us angrily, *"Mottainai!"* This translates roughly as "What a waste!"

The okoge was to be saved and shared with everyone over informal tea at midmorning. The rice starch went to feed the koi in the small pond behind our kitchen. The fish gathered hungrily when they saw us approach each day. This was a great treat for them.

I am still a pitiful, wasteful person. "Mottainai" rings in my ears.

LAURIE SENAUKE

I Will Not Abandon You

I'VE BEEN MARRIED to Laurie since 1989. We have lived together at Berkeley Zen Center since then. We raised our children Silvie and Alexander here and watched them go out into the world. We have a fortunate marriage and a fortunate life.

There are always people in our lives whose needs appear overwhelming. Sometimes those needs are overwhelming for the person experiencing them and for others who try to help them meet those needs. Friends, neighbors, loved ones knock on our door looking for assistance of various kinds at various times. Within our limited material means, we offer what we can, even when it is not nearly enough. But we can always—or almost always—give our care and attention. We can accompany people. We can listen.

Laurie came up with this phrase—words we can share explicitly or implicitly: *I will not abandon you.* This is what Thich Nhat Hanh describes as a "northstar precept"—a principle we have come to in our own words that expresses the bodhisattva's vow to awaken with all beings.

I will not abandon you. I may not be able to give you all that you need or think you need, but I will not turn away from you. In the hardest times, in the middle of the night, you can call me and I will do my best to hold your grief and fear. At least I can do that.

THE NATURE OF SUFFERING

When I rant about the conditions of my life or somebody's actions toward me or toward another, Laurie has a simple and irrefutable response. "You are suffering because you want things to be different from how they are." This is the boiled-down essence of *dukkha*.

Still I seem to need to do a bit of ranting from time to time. Not to convince Laurie that I am correct in my view. Not to convince myself, but just to hear myself say the words, to let the anger vent properly. This anger or dissatisfaction has power when it bounces around within me. Expressed in words, the power dissipates. An hour later I can be back at zero.

ATTACHMENT

Laurie and I were driving to Marin County to do an errand in the midst of the COVID-19 pandemic. We were talking about our children, Silvie and Alexander. Alex had spent the last five months at Sogenji, Shodo Harada Roshi's monastery in Okayama, Japan. He seemed to be enjoying the rigorous schedule and intimate practice there. Silvie was in Chicago consulting with the Department of Family and Support Services. Of course, she was working from home, but she could go out to shop and get exercise. Actually, both our kids seemed to be engaged, buoyant, and in good health. Yet, they were far away and we worried about them.

Laurie offhandedly said something that caught my attention: "The kids still occupy at least half of my psyche." I realize that is true for me, too, though my worry operates under the surface of day-to-day concerns. I think both of us imagined that when the kids grew into adulthood, free from their immediate dependence on us as parents, the burden of attachment would lessen. Instead, it seems that in some ways the stakes are higher. My attachment to their success—not material success but actual happiness—is even stronger. I wonder what a real Buddhist would think about this?

THIS MOMENT

Laurie and I were discussing a Zen talk where I heard the proposition that "everything is perfect," which did not sit easily with me. Laurie proposed an alternative formulation: "This moment has in it everything I need in order to wake up." Yes.

SANTA CLAUS AND THE MIND-ONLY SCHOOL OF BUDDHISM

During the pandemic, Laurie and I regularly read and discussed the *Lankavatara Sutra*. This is an early Buddhist classic text, a rigorous philosophical dialogue between Shakyamuni Buddha and his disciple Mahamati, about the nature of existence, nonexistence, and awakening. It was handed down by Bodhidharma, the First Ancestor of Zen, and is cherished and foundational to the Yogacara, or Mind-Only School, which is the basis of Zen.

It proposes that beings and things neither exist nor do they not exist; that what we see and take for "real" is inevitably a projection of our mind, an imputation based on previous experience. As we wrestled with the question of whether there is any form existent beyond perception, Laurie said, "Well, this is like asking: Is there a Santa Claus?"

VENERABLE SHENG YEN

Regulate Your Life

MASTER SHENG YEN was the founder of Dharma Drum Mountain, one of the "Four Mountains" of contemporary Buddhism in Taiwan, with lineage in both the Rinzai and Soto traditions. I knew of him in the 1980s as the teacher at a Chan center in Elmhurst, Queens, in New York City. Ron Nestor from Berkeley Zen Center sat several *sesshins* with him in Elmhurst, so we invited Master Sheng Yen to give a talk at BZC when it was convenient in his travels.

This must have been in 1989, on a weekday evening. The zendo was full. Sojun Roshi was in his abbot's seat. Master Sheng Yen lectured from the teacher's seat. As is often the case—then and now—I have no recollection of his talk. It was followed by questions and answers from the gathered students. Laurie asked one of those archetypal Zen questions: "What is the most important thing for a lay practitioner to remember?"

The Master answered, "Regulate your life."

For thirty years since, I've been trying to regulate my life. I've also been thinking about what that means. *Regulate* is a rich word. The *Oxford English Dictionary* says it means to "control or maintain the rate or speed of a machine or process so that it operates properly." The Latin root *reg* means "rule," as in the rule of a king. You could say that a king's job is to make sure that the nation runs harmoniously. There is also the sense of a monastic rule, an "institutionalized religious practice or movement" in which order members follow a formal pattern of prayer, work, and life. Regulate brings to mind the word *regular*—in common parlance, "normal or ordinary, not special." Which reminds me of a Zen dialogue from China's Tang dynasty: Joshu asked Master Nansen, "What is the Way?" Nansen replied, "Ordinary mind is the Way." And so we have come full circle. Nansen tells Joshu to regulate his life, put it in order.

I will keep trying.

THICH NHAT HANH

Mindfulness Must Be Engaged

THICH NHAT HANH always wore the simple brown robes of a monk. He walked and spoke mindfully as a Zen teacher, poet, and bridge between the world's faiths. But the strength of steel lay just below his placid surface. The Zen teacher Richard Baker described Thich Nhat Hanh as "a cross between a cloud, a snail, and piece of heavy machinery—a true religious presence."[6]

When I started working at the Buddhist Peace Fellowship, I posted a broadside over my desk with an excerpt from Thich Nhat Hanh's book *Peace Is Every Step*. In part it read,

> Mindfulness must be engaged. Once there is seeing, there must be acting. Otherwise, what is the use of seeing? We must be aware of the real problems of the world. Then, with mindfulness, we will know what to do and what not to do to be of help. . . . Are you planting seeds of joy and peace? I try to do that with every step. Peace is every step. Shall we continue the journey?[7]

The disarmingly straightforward wisdom of Thich Nhat Hanh was tempered in Vietnam's anticolonial struggle against the French and the devastation of the US war that followed. In the face of these conflicts, Thich Nhat Hanh brought a nonviolent movement to the Buddhist monasteries and created the School of Youth for Social Service, a cohort of Buddhist peace workers in rural villages of Vietnam.

"So many of our villages were being bombed," Thich Nhat Hanh said. "Along with my monastic brothers and sisters, I had to decide what to do. Should we continue to practice in our monasteries, or should we leave the meditation halls in order to help the people who were suffering under the bombs? After careful reflection, we decided to do both—to go out and help people and to do so in mindfulness. We called it 'engaged Buddhism.'"[8]

In the late 1960s, Thich Nhat Hanh, familiarly known as Thay, was exiled from Vietnam—an exile that continued until 2005. Mistrusted by both the communists and nationalists in his own country, he steered a middle way of Buddhist-based nonviolence. In the United States he found like-minded comrades in Dr. Martin Luther King Jr., Thomas Merton, the radical Catholic Berrigan brothers, Western Buddhist teachers and students, and activists within the nonviolent circle of the Fellowship of Reconciliation and the Buddhist Peace Fellowship.

I began reading Thay's books in the 1980s, starting with *The Miracle of Mindfulness* and then *Being Peace*. After *Being*

Peace, the stream of published words by Thay became a wide river, with brilliant commentaries on classic Theravada and Mahayana sutras, radical reinterpretations of the bodhisattva precepts, and Buddhist social commentary on our troubled modern world. As they rolled off the presses, his books were eagerly read by so many of us in the Buddhist community.

As director of the BPF, I was asked by Thay to organize biennial talks at the Berkeley Community Theater, which accommodated four thousand people. The first talk I organized was in April 1991, in the immediate aftermath of Desert Storm, the first US war against Saddam Hussein's Iraq following its invasion of Kuwait, and the police beating of Rodney King, a Black man, in Los Angeles.

I was struck by Thay's comments that night. He spoke of his deep anger over the war in Kuwait and the beating of King, both of which seemed to trigger for him painful memories of the war in Vietnam and the brutal ignorance of US oppression. He said he had considered canceling his tour, with all its retreats and dharma events.

His words revealed to me that Thay wasn't an unreachable saint but a man with raw feelings. Then he shared that he'd meditated on his own reactivity and realized that he had to continue his tour as planned, because these oppressors and victims—the police, Rodney King, US soldiers, Iraqis, and all their government leaders—were neither different from nor distant from himself.

That same week, in a *Los Angeles Times* op-ed, Thich Nhat Hanh wrote,

> Looking more deeply, I was able to see that the policemen who were beating Rodney King were also myself. Why were they doing that? Because our society is full of hatred and violence. Everything is like a bomb ready to explode, and we are part of that bomb. We are coresponsible for that bomb. That is why I saw myself as the policemen beating the driver. We all are these policemen.[9]

This insight about interdependence is what I have learned from Thich Nhat Hanh. It flows from how he has taught and walked in the world, but it is not a special vision of his own. Such insight appears to Buddhist and spiritual teachers of all lands and ages. It comes from poets and seers. Walt Whitman wrote: "I am large, I contain multitudes." Let us strive to be like Thay—that is, to be truly human, our basic selves.

SANTIKARO

The Incinerator of Defilement

SANTIKARO UPASAKA, a.k.a. Robert Larson, was a monk in the Thai Theravada tradition for nearly twenty years. He was a disciple and translator for the great teacher Ajahn Buddhadasa at Suan Mokkh in Southern Thailand, where he led the monthly meditation retreats for many years. Santikaro now resides at Liberation Park in Norwalk, Wisconsin. He leads retreats there, elsewhere in the United States, and in Thailand.

I met Santikaro at conferences of the International Network of Engaged Buddhists in the early 1990s, and our connection blossomed into a close friendship between us and with my family in Berkeley, where he has been a frequent visitor. Our conversations have been wide-ranging, but there is a particular teaching Santikaro shared from his teacher Buddhadasa that has guided me since I first heard it. It is his gloss on a line from *Dhammapada* 184: "Patience is the supreme incinerator of defilements."

Burning up all hindrances by the application of patience (*kshanti*). Patience was never my strong suit, but I have come to value it above all the *paramitas*, or perfections. We cultivate patience as we sit zazen, facing the wall, facing ourselves, day by day. Patience is the ability to endure what we imagine to be unendurable. We may survive the ordeal, or we may not. Either way, patience is required. The practice of patience extends our capacity to meet suffering and to include it in the everyday workings of life.

SULAK SIVARAKSA

Seeds of Peace

I FIRST HEARD ABOUT Ajahn Sulak Sivaraksa while I was working at Parallax Press in 1990. I had an opportunity to read his book *Seeds of Peace: A Buddhist Vision for Renewing Society* as it was going through the editing process. His was the clearest articulation of engaged Buddhism I had come across. But, more to the point, the example of his activity as an engaged Buddhist has been a model and resource over more than thirty years.

In the spring of 1992, following a 1991 military coup in Thailand, Sulak fled the country when lèse-majesté charges were filed against him for defaming the military regime and the Thai monarchy. Escaping Asia by way of Europe and the United States, Sulak arrived at our house in Berkeley and stayed with us for several months. It was there we began working on his book *Loyalty Demands Dissent: Autobiography of an Engaged Buddhist.*

During that period, I was working at Buddhist Peace Fellowship, preparing to travel to Thailand to attend my first

International Network of Engaged Buddhists conference, the organization Sulak had founded several years earlier. I remember that, with baggage in hand, I left my home on Russell Street in Berkeley with Sulak bidding me farewell, to arrive twenty hours later at his comfortable home in the Bang Rak district of Bangkok, a home he would not be able to return to for another six months.

Our friendship has endured for many years, across continents, despite arguments and conflicts, which are not relevant here. Apart from my root teacher Sojun Roshi, no one has been more pivotal in my connection to the wide Buddhist world than Ajahn Sulak. So many of his friends and acolytes have become my working partners and close friends. His writing and thinking continue to influence me. His provocations still hit their mark, for friends and opponents alike.

OUR HEROES' FAILURES

I've looked back through my old notebooks, but I cannot find the occasion on which Sulak spoke of our great spiritual teachers and heroes as failures. He was, of course, intentionally provocative, truly not disparaging. Sulak was keenly aware that these teachers and leaders set a very high bar for themselves and for us. Yet, there are truths to be considered. Consider Socrates, Jesus Christ, Joan of Arc, Abraham Lincoln and leaping ahead to Gandhi, John F. Kennedy, Dr. Martin Luther King Jr., Thich Nhat Hanh, the Dalai Lama. Each was shaped and tempered by challenges and failures. Their work may be incomplete, despite their working tirelessly to achieve their larger vision of freedom. Many of them paid for their efforts with their life-blood. Yet these figures continue to inspire us, quite apart from our limited views of success and failure. To cite a capping verse by Bob Dylan, they know "there's no success like failure. And that failure's no success at all."

ROBERT AITKEN

Dharma Words

ZEN MASTER ROBERT AITKEN was one of the found-ers of Buddhist Peace Fellowship. I am grateful for the close connection that developed between us over twenty years. Bodhidharma said that Zen is "a special transmission out-side the scriptures, not founded upon words and letters." Bodhidharma would have to add a codicil for Robert Aitken: the gecko's call, the nightingale's song are nothing other than scriptures, words, and letters.

Aitken Roshi loved words and literature as a manifes-tation of dharma. He recognized that love in others. One steamy afternoon at Sulak Sivaraksa's place in Thailand, Aitken Roshi suggested to me that as I was a person with an affinity for language, I might consider koan study. Of course, he snookered me, and I spent a good many months at his direction wrangling with the koan Mu, which is beyond the realm of words. Mu, by the way, is the first case in Master Wu-men's *Gateless Barrier,* a classic collection of seemingly paradoxical enlightening stories or koans studied in the Zen tradition. The case, very simply put, is itself a tall barrier for many students, myself included.

> A monk asked Chao-chou, "Has the dog Buddha-nature or not?"
> Chao-chou said, "Mu."[10]

Mu means "no," but of course, the question and answer are not so simple—not susceptible to words or linguistic acuity.

At the second Buddhist Peace Fellowship institute in 1992, Aitken Roshi gave a series of talks on the *paramitas*, or perfections, each morning after meditation and before breakfast. These talks, along with some of our group discussion, were later edited into his book *The Practice of Perfection*. It was a wonderful way to begin our daily work. For the remainder of the day, Roshi studied and rested, joined some of the workshops, but mostly I remember him seeing a steady stream of students who had heard he was visiting Oakland. By this point in his life, he lived mostly in Hawaii, straying to the mainland once or twice a year. On this visit, students came from all corners of the Bay Area and beyond, meeting him formally and informally in his room, over meals, or walking the grounds of the down-at-the-heels Catholic retreat center where we gathered.

One night, well into our week together, I woke at about three in the morning to use the bathroom. Walking back, I seemed to hear voices from farther down the hall. Zeroing in on the sound, I recognized the deep, dry sound of Aitken Roshi's voice addressing a point of dharma with some urgency. My god! Did his students (I wasn't one at the time) never leave him alone? *Dokusan* at 3:00 a.m.! Let the old guy get some sleep.

Who was it? I padded closer to the door. There was no dialogue. Only Roshi's measured sentences rolled forth. Then repeated with a small shift of wording or emphasis. Words on *virya paramita*, the perfection of zeal or energy—his talk for later that morning. I was astonished, somewhat relieved, and went back to bed.

This moment—bare feet in the darkened hallway, dharma words late at night—is still clear and potent for me. Roshi's expression of virya paramita, almost secretly practiced, using it all up and replenishing himself. Don't rely on text already written; rather, weigh each word. What do I really think? What do I really mean? Keep polishing.

MAHA GHOSANANDA

What Is the Most Important Thing?

IN AUTUMN 1992 about forty of us, mostly from across Asia, took the night train from Bangkok to Chiang Mai, freezing all night in the excessive air-conditioning, eventually arriving in that northern city at dawn. Open vans took us to Wat Umong, the "tunnel temple" at the foot of Doi Suthep to the west of the city. This was my first trip to Thailand, and my first International Network of Engaged Buddhists (INEB) conference. The friends I traveled with and met there have been my close dharma brothers and sisters ever since.

An aging monk, diminutive and somewhat androgynous, took center stage in his orange robes. He spoke briskly, in low tones. The smile on his face was audible. This was the first time I heard Maha Ghosananda, Cambodian patriarch in exile, teach.

Later, I met with Bhante Ghosananda numerous times throughout the 1990s—both at INEB conferences and in the Bay Area. Bhante traveled alone, and his students and supporters often did not know where he was or where he was going. From time to time, someone would call and ask if I had seen Bhante. "We think he is headed to San Francisco." And he would show up in a day or two, completely calm, laughing easily, walking, floating two inches above the ground, and always moving forward.

Back to Chiang Mai in 1992. Maha Ghosananda made himself comfortable sitting onstage. He beamed at the assembly and asked, "What is the most important thing?" He called on young monks, on elders, on the INEB notables. Each threw out a good answer and each was met with a disappointed nod of the head. This went on for twenty minutes. Finally, Bhante said, "The most important thing is eating." In his book *Step by Step* Maha Ghosananda explains:

Life is eating and drinking through all of our senses. And life is keeping from being eaten. What eats us? Time! What is time? Time is living in the past or living in the future, feeding on the emotions. Beings who can say that they are mentally healthy for even one minute are rare in the world. Most of us suffer from clinging to pleasant, unpleasant, and neutral feelings, and from hunger and thirst. Most living beings have to eat and drink every second through their eyes, ears, nose, tongue, skin, and nerves. We eat twenty-four hours a day without stopping! We crave food for the body, food for feeling, food for volitional action, and food for rebirth. We are what we eat. We are the world, and we eat the world . . .

Time is also an eater. In traditional Cambodian stories, there is often a giant with many mouths who eats everything. This giant is time. If you eat time, you gain nirvana. You can eat time by living in the moment. When you live just in this moment, time cannot eat you.[11]

UNWRAPPING A MONK

One morning in 1996 I received a call at home from a monk at Nagara Dhamma Temple, a Cambodian *vihara* (monastery) in San Francisco's Sunset district. He explained that Maha Ghosananda was there and wanted to visit with me in Berkeley. I was surprised, but in the background I heard Bhante Ghosananda shout, "Now!"

Since it was still morning, Laurie and I scrambled to make a lunch before noon to offer the two monks. They made it to Berkeley just in time to eat. After lunch, Ghosananda led me into my office. He was in his early eighties then. In all his saffron robes he appeared physically substantial, with a look of grandmotherly sweetness. But in my office, he began to disrobe, shedding layer after layer of cloth until I saw a very slight old man in his saffron underwear.

Under all his robes he had a thin vest with numerous pockets, which he began to explore. Many of these pockets held packets of currency in varying denominations from different countries. It is worth noting that according to the Theravada *vinaya* (the code of monastic discipline—227 rules for monks, 311 for nuns), monks were not supposed to handle money. But Maha Ghosananda always seemed to have his own rules and his own inviolable purity of spirit. Anyway, he kept pulling out these packets, replacing them, and looking further until he came to a wad of US money, mostly in fifties and hundreds. Triumphantly he waved the bills at me and said, "This is for INEB. Please get it to them."

I took the money and bowed to him. Then Bhante Ghosananda began to rewrap himself in all those layers of cloth. When he was done, he smiled, gathered up his attending monk and left. A brush with greatness.

BERNIE TETSUGEN
GLASSMAN

Three Tenets

I CAN'T RECALL when I first heard about Bernie Glassman and the Greyston Bakery he built in a downtrodden district of Yonkers, New York. I had read Glassman's early books, three volumes called *On Zen Practice* in collaboration with his teacher Taizan Maezumi Roshi of Zen Center of Los Angeles. In 1979 he moved back to his native New York City. By 1982 the bakery was up and running, and Glassman Roshi became a burgeoning social entrepreneur.

In January 1994 Bernie spent his fifty-fifth birthday on retreat in Washington, DC, reflecting on how best to serve the hungry, the poor, the ill and rejected. The vision of a Zen Peacemaker Order emerged. With his wife, Sandra Jishu Holmes, Bernie set out to build it. They asked themselves and their friends, "What forms can we create in modern life that will be conducive to seeing the oneness of life? What are the forms that will make it easier to experience interconnectedness?"

Bernie and I met while I was working at Buddhist Peace Fellowship, and I became intermittently involved with the Zen Peacemakers later in the decade. Meanwhile, Bernie's visionary social service organization, the Greyston Mandala, expanded to include the bakery, housing and support systems for families moving out of homelessness; Maitri House, which helped people with HIV/AIDS; Bearing Witness retreats at the Nazi death camp Auschwitz-Birkenau and elsewhere; and street retreats in Washington DC, New York, Seattle, Denver, LA, and cities across Europe, where the Zen Peacemaker Order remains strong.

The various Peacemaker organizations kept evolving, devolving, dissolving, and regrouping over the years. Bernie, photographer Peter Cunningham, and their clown teacher Mr. YooWho—Moshe Cohen—created the Order of Disorder, in its own way an accurate expression of Bernie's world. But all of this impermanence, change, and entropy was actually the point. Standing in the middle of it all was Bernie. There are Yiddish words to describe him: *mensch*—an upright, honorable man; *shtarker*—a strong man, brave, and a little *meshuggeneh*—meaning crazy or not entirely practical (to say the least).

Bernie, Jishu, and their Peacemaker circle articulated a core teaching at the center of their work:

THE THREE TENETS

Not Knowing—thereby giving up fixed ideas about ourselves and the universe

    Bearing Witness—to the joy and suffering of the world

    Loving Action—for ourselves and the world

WHAT IS ENLIGHTENMENT?

Bernie wrote that Kukai, or Kōbō-Daishi as he was post-humously named (774–835, the founder of Japan's esoteric Shingon Sect), said that one can tell the depth of a person's enlightenment by how they serve others. This resonates with me as an operative standard for so-called "enlightenment," something that is an action rather than an experience. But I have spent hours trying to track down this quotation from Kukai. If you know the source, please write me.

THAT'S JUST MY OPINION, MAN

In the late 1990s, the Coen brothers' film *The Big Lebowski* introduced many of us to "The Dude" and his anarchic take on life, including the unanswerable comeback, "That's just, you know, like, your opinion, man." In time, Bernie became close friends with Jeff Bridges, the actor who perfectly embodied the Dude. From the Dude's unique expressions Bernie created a kind of koan system for the latest incarnation of his engaged Zen training. For didactic purposes, Bernie inverted the Dude's expression, turning it on himself: "That's just my opinion, man."

What occurs to me is that the Dude is expressing the fundamental principle of Yogacara Buddhism—that what we think of as the world is constructed from the interaction of our senses, our mind, and our storehouse consciousness containing seeds of everything we have ever experienced. There is no objective reality, just a world of subjectivity—an opinion. In the fall 2013 issue of *Naropa Magazine*, the journalist Lindsay Michko wrote,

> Abandoning the "standard" lecture format, Glassman took audience questions first, scribbling them down until he had filled a sheet of paper, explaining, "Our meal will be our discussion. What are the ingredients? Our questions . . . I like questions. I don't like answers—answers tend to kill the discussion."
>
> . . . Amidst his wise pieces of advice, Glassman continued to remind us that everything is only an opinion. "Don't let anyone give you a truth, man. There are no truths, just opinions."

No truths, just opinions. Or statistical probability, as we think about scientific "truth." So, Shakyamuni Buddha's core teaching of the Four Noble Truths becomes the Four Noble Opinions. Of course, this does get me to pause and think. In a sense, this is a contemporary condensation of the Mind-Only School of early Mahayana Buddhism. To quote a line from the *Lankavatara Sutra*: "To see things as they really are means to transcend what are nothing but perceptions of your own mind."

Still, I have tried to argue with Bernie that some things are not opinions—like the bombing of Hiroshima, climate change, or, say, gravity—and I've run up against the Dude's unscalable wall, "That's just, like, your opinion, man." This is what the Zen scholar D. T. Suzuki meant when he wrote, "The *koan* is an iron wall standing in the way and threatening to overcome one's every intellectual effort to pass." At last, it is left to each of us to plunge into the heart of imponderable reality. But that's just my opinion, man.

NELSON FOSTER

You Can't Stay Anywhere

NELSON FOSTER is the teacher at Ring of Bone Zendo on San Juan Ridge in the foothills of California's Sierras. In the course of Zen training with Robert Aitken, Nelson was one of the founders of Buddhist Peace Fellowship on the front porch of the old Maui Zendo in 1978. Relying on Nelson's Buddhist wisdom, his background as an organizer for the American Friends Service Committee, and his extensive experience as a careful editor, I turned to him for guidance while I was working at BPF.

As executive director, I had a regular column in each issue of *Turning Wheel*, BPF's quarterly journal. This was my opportunity to reflect on BPF's activities, on the wider world of engaged Buddhism, and on the Buddha's necessary teachings. One evening in the mid-90s I got a phone call at home from Nelson, which was a rare event. After the customary civilities, Nelson got down to business. In my latest column, I had carelessly used a clichéd expression, something about "staying in the present." Nelson's message was simple and blunt: "You can't stay anywhere." Impermanence, change, *anicca* is not just an idea, it is at the heart of the Buddha's teachings. Nelson's call was a wake-up for me.

JOSEPH GOLDSTEIN

Words in the Present

WHILE I WAS WORKING at Buddhist Peace Fellowship, we were fortunate to have the support of numerous dharma teachers who would do benefit events for us. In January 1997 Joseph Goldstein was kind enough to offer a public talk in the beautiful sanctuary of St. John's Presbyterian Church in Berkeley. Words that stay with me from that evening were Joseph's description of a challenging practice of right speech he had tried for a time. Joseph said,

> The practice is easy to recount and difficult to accomplish. Simply put, one tries never to say anything about someone else who is not present. When you think about it, this eliminates a large percentage of our verbal activity. Think about it. Better yet, try it for a single day.

I try this practice from time to time. It's pretty hard. More practically and more often, I check myself to make sure that

I would be willing to say face-to-face what I might be saying about someone outside their presence. It is often better, as Katagiri Roshi advised, to "keep your mouth shut and look directly at impermanence!"

JARVIS MASTERS

A Buddhist on Death Row

JARVIS JAY MASTERS, C35169, an innocent man resid-
ing on East Block, San Quentin State Prison's death row,
has been my friend since 1997. A Buddhist practitioner, he
had been publishing vivid articles in *Turning Wheel*, Buddhist Peace Fellowship's quarterly journal, when we met. My
friend Melody Ermachild Chavis, who was Jarvis's private
investigator and a member of Berkeley Zen Center, encouraged me to visit him. So I did, and I still do.

I can't point to particular phrases or turning words spoken between us, but my whole relationship with Jarvis is
located in words. First of all, he is a fine writer. As to words
between us, there have been years of noncontact visits with
black telephone handsets connecting us across two sides
of a grimy plexiglass window; knee to knee in small legal
interview cages, talking, laughing, arguing; Global Tel
Link phone calls, with the din of death-row voices making
it hard to hear; notes and letters; messages from common
friends.

At the end of our visits, I walk out into the crisp San Francisco Bay air and Jarvis is escorted back to his cell on East Block. I've never seen East Block; I can't imagine his life there or in his previous three decades of solitary confinement in San Quentin's Adjustment Center. Nor can I imagine his life before prison—years of foster care and more years in the notorious California Youth Authority.

Aside from my love for Jarvis and my admiration for a spirit and practice unbroken by more than half a life on death row, there is one essential teaching I have received from him. Each individual wishes to make their own decisions in life. Privileged people, like myself, take autonomy for granted. People like Jarvis who have been marginalized by virtue of race, economics, imprisonment, or any number of other factors often find that decisions about their lives are made by others—patriarchal powers, the state, corporations, and so on. In Jarvis Masters's case, he has lived much of his life in an environment of social control. Prison, of course, is the perfection of social control.

The lessons of autonomy I've had from Jarvis have been hard learned, mistake by mistake. Mostly my mistakes have involved speaking for Jarvis before checking with him about what he might wish me to write or say or whether I should say anything at all. I grew up with the idea that speech is free and the words I speak belong to me—that I could say whatever I thought. In an extended sense, this is part of the meaning of the seventh bodhisattva precept: "Not praising self at the expense of others." To appropriate the words or actions of another is (often unconsciously) to feel superior to that other person, that one has an unearned superiority permitting that appropriation.

What I have learned is that words and stories about another's life belong, first of all, to that person. We borrow them only with their permission. More so when that person—a prisoner, a victim, a person on the margins of society, a friend—does not have access to channels of communication that I might have by virtue of gender, race, education, and so on. As I say, I have learned this the hard way. I still have a ways to go.

NOTE: Jarvis is a brilliant writer and storyteller. His two books are *Finding Freedom: How Death Row Broke and Opened My Heart* (new edition from Shambhala Publications, 2020) and *That Bird Has My Wings: The Autobiography of an Innocent Man on Death Row* (Harper-One, 2009). Best-selling author David Sheff worked with Jarvis on a 2020 memoir, published in 2020 by Simon & Schuster: *The Buddhist on Death Row: How One Man Found Light in the Darkest Place.*

SHODO HARADA

Encounters

IN THE LATE 1990s, Zen friends were encouraging me to experience practice with Shodo Harada, the teacher at Sogenji/One Drop Zendo in Okayama, Japan, and at Tahoma Zen Center on Whidbey Island, Washington. Harada Roshi and his associate Daichi Priscilla Storandt—familiarly known as Chisan—have been wise teachers for me over more than twenty years. My son Alex (dharma name, Genpo) is their student and practiced as a monk at Sogenji for nearly two years.

I can't remember what finally moved me to practice with Harada Roshi, but it was probably around 1998 or 1999—a rainy, cold February in the Northwest. This was before they had built the Tahoma monastery, so *sesshin* was in a sprawling ranch house next door, which is now Enso House, Tahoma's hospice facility. Practice with Roshi is brisk and intense. "Cut away, cut away" all extraneous thinking, dualism, attachments. Arrive at the serene essence. Then move forward from that place.

In our first *sanzen*—formal interview between teacher and student—Roshi said, "Show me your breath." I just laughed because I couldn't do it. His energy was too strong for me to find my composure, so I had to admit it. He sat upright with a teaching stick resting in his lap and took a deep breath, letting it out audibly with a deep, slow growl—*muuuu* . . . I was drawn into this breath, this rhythm. We did this together in the sanzen room, just breathing together for hours, which were really two or three minutes. He rang the bell. I bowed and left the room.

The following year the Tahoma community moved into their monastery on Whidbey Island. It was still kind of rough and ready, but at least I knew the ropes. The first night in sanzen I asked Harada Roshi how he wanted me to work with him. My training was Soto Zen and I had come to a strong Rinzai teacher. "Do you want me to be working on a koan?" Koan introspection was his customary teaching. He shook his head and in his deep, gravelly voice said, "No, you already have your practice." That part was in English. He spoke briefly in Japanese, which Chisan, sitting in the sanzen room, translated: "Just bring yourself completely to sanzen!" Oh, that's all.

The next year. February again; blustery, chilling weather. I think I arrived already depleted. Everyone, including Harada Roshi, got sick. Me too. Chills and muscle aches. There was no way and nowhere to get warm. In sanzen Roshi read my energy and mood. He spoke in the kindest way. "Hozan-san, you must take care of your health and body. The world needs you. There is much work to do. Help the world."

MEMORIAL SLOAN KETTERING

In the spring of 2017, my friend Jon Sholle was diagnosed with a rare and very aggressive skin cancer. We had been very close from 1962, ninth grade in Great Neck, New York. We played music together over all these years, but from the start, Jon was an intuitive master of the guitar and every other instrument he picked up. He was incredibly smart, funny, warm, and troubled too. He took up Zen practice, I think at my example, and I introduced him to Harada Roshi. Over his fifteen years of daily practice, Jon—or Tanzan, his dharma name—was devoted to zazen and committed to his teacher Harada Roshi. Those years of practice settled his inner life and his family. He had a glimpse of peace.

By late summer the cancer had advanced and manifested as several large tumors that were visible and growing quickly. Aside from other medical approaches, these needed to be removed surgically. One night I got a call from Chisan in Japan. She said that she and Roshi were flying to the United States for sesshin at Tahoma and wanted to visit Tanzan on the other side of the country in New York City. I said that was wonderful, and Chisan replied, "We need you to drive us." Of course.

So, two weeks later, the day after Jon's surgery, I met Roshi and Chisan at San Francisco International Airport when they came off their flight from Japan. We immediately boarded a flight to Newark, where I rented a car. Somewhere around two in the morning we fell into our respective beds at a Newark motel. A few hours later we were awake and off to Sloan Kettering in the morning traffic. Jon was still bandaged and medicated from a long surgery the day before. But he beamed with joy through his tears on seeing us.

All morning they spoke about the dharma. Bearing the unbearable. How to actually face one's approaching death, doing all one can to live fully while alive but not ignoring what was inevitable and near. By midday, Jon was very tired, and the teachers needed to catch an afternoon flight to Seattle. Sesshin at Tahoma would begin that night. So we got back in the car, back in the Manhattan traffic, and returned to Newark airport. I left Roshi and Chisan with bows and hugs. They caught their flight and I returned to the hospital to be with Jon and his wife Betty.

As I said of Aitken Roshi—and one could just as well say of Shunryu Suzuki Roshi, Katagiri Roshi, Maezumi Roshi, and many other respected elders—they use themselves up on our behalf. This is their expression of the bodhisattva vows.

> Sentient beings are numberless; I vow to save them
> Delusions are inexhaustible; I vow to end them.
> Dharma gates are boundless; I vow to enter them.
> The Buddha's way is unsurpassable; I vow to accomplish it.

That these dear teachers would fly across the continent and back to spend three hours with an ailing student is almost unimaginable in our wounded, spinning world. They had no hesitation, just as I did not hesitate to go and help them. The Buddha's way is love. This was an act of love.

SEISHO MAYLIE SCOTT

Devotedly Do

MY DHARMA SISTER Maylie Scott—Kushin Seisho, Vast Mind, Clearly Shining—died in May 2001 at Rin Shin-ji, Forest Heart Zen Temple in Arcata, California. She began her practice of Zen with Sojun Mel Weitsman in 1971 and received dharma transmission together with me at Tassajara in 1998. Her watchwords were "devotedly do."

Maylie was like a tree—feet firmly on the ground, graying head and smile reaching toward the sky. For fifteen years I relied on Maylie for unsentimental clarity and heart. She and I shared the *tanto* seat at BZC, serving as "heads of practice" under Sojun Roshi.

As a dharma sister, Maylie was always willing to listen fully, to challenge assumptions—even her own—and to point again and again to the strength of zazen. In life and in death, she showed us how to bear the unbearable.

We worked together at Buddhist Peace Fellowship, at the Federal Correctional Institution in Dublin, California, and in the endlessly frustrating struggle against American militarism. Maylie led the way. She was arrested again and again blocking railway tracks at the Concord Naval Weapons Station. She worked with AIDS patients and fed homeless people. She was the first mentor for Buddhist Peace Fellowship's Buddhist Alliance for Social Engagement programs (which ran from 1990 to 2005 in the San Francisco Bay Area) and served tirelessly on the BPF board. But her foundational practice was showing up for zazen every day, sometimes twice a day at BZC, a shining example of dedicated practice.

In the years since her death, I have found myself doing many of the things that Maylie set in motion. Cooking meals at the Berkeley homeless shelter. Teaching women prisoners at the federal prison in Dublin. Participating in nonviolent civil disobedience. Visiting and teaching at the Arcata Zen group. I try to remember to meet each being as a buddha and to "devotedly do" as she did.

BHANTE SUHITA DHARMA

A Cloud, a Buffalo

SOMETIMES, WITHOUT A WORD, a person can turn you. Bhante Suhita Dharma was such a person. A floating cloud, a determined buffalo. In the early 1990s, while I was at Buddhist Peace Fellowship, I heard about an African American monk who had founded the Metta Vihara hospice in a poor section of Richmond, California. This was a home for people with HIV/AIDS, many of whom were addicts or previously incarcerated—those who often fell off the edges of society. I went numerous times to visit and talk with him, and we became better acquainted as *kalyanamitta*, spiritual friends. This was Bhante's lifelong practice, just to walk alongside those whose lives were marked by suffering.

In 2005, Suhita Dharma joined the staff of Buddhist Peace Fellowship as the prison program coordinator and codirector of the Coming Home Project, helping former prisoners find stability in a world beyond the prison walls. For a time he was my downstairs neighbor at Berkeley Zen Center, living his quiet monk's way in our community.

Born in Texas and raised in the Bay Area, he entered a Trappist monastery at the age of fifteen as Brother Anthony. Turning toward Buddhism without ever rejecting his Catholic monastic roots, Bhante was the first African American to receive full ordination in Theravada, Mahayana, and Vajrayana traditions.

The Most Venerable Suhita Dharma Mahathero was a monk for fifty-eight years. Unexpectedly, he entered final nirvana on December 28, 2013, at Chua Dieu Phap Temple in San Gabriel, California. It is hard to describe someone who embodies formlessness, cloudlike. This is not to say that he was ever less than human or, for that matter, more than human. Though trained in the practices and rituals of numerous monastic practices, Bhante Suhita radiated a simple, warm light. When I was with him, the joy he experienced as a young Trappist was always close at hand. I saw that same joy on his fellow monks' faces when he spoke with them. That joy remained the sign of his life.

Bhante, wherever you are, I wish for you and all beings "Blessings of the Triple Gem."

NOTE: A fuller sketch of Bhante Suhita's life by his close friend Mushim Ikeda can be found at https://buddhistpeacefellowship .org/floating-onward-honoring-venerable-bhante-suhita-dharma/.

DAJIAN HUINENG

Sentient Beings of My Mind

MASTER HUINENG (638–713 CE) is known as the Sixth Ancestor of Chinese Zen, following Bodhidharma, the First Ancestor. Huineng is the presumptive author of the *Platform Sutra*, one of the few scriptures composed outside of India taken to be words of a buddha. About fifteen years ago, I wrote a novel that straddles the life of Huineng and China during the Cultural Revolution. I really enjoyed researching both historical periods—Huineng's life in the Tang dynasty, digging into various texts, translations, and scholarly papers, and the Cultural Revolution, with political turmoil and upheaval that went far beyond my own activist experience in the 1960s. While there are parts of the novel I think are pretty good, it now lives in a cozy space on my laptop's hard drive.

The *Platform Sutra's* sixth chapter, "On Repentance," is Master Huineng's "formless" ceremony of repentance and renewal, following the model of a Buddhist ordination. In this chapter Huineng presents his version of the four bodhisattva vows. In our centers and temples, the first vow is like this: *Sentient beings are numberless; I vow to save them.* Huineng's version adds a few simple words: *Sentient beings of my mind are numberless; I vow to save them all.*

These few words are deeply meaningful to me. First, that I am included within the population of numberless beings. Second, that rebirth—in terms we often discuss in Zen—is moment by moment for each of us. Think about the Buddhist cosmology's six realms: humans, gods, fighting demons, hungry ghosts, animals, and hell-dwellers. As we move through various mental and emotional states, we are immediately born in these and countless other realms. At that moment, this is a sentient being of my mind: a lost child, a woman with no place to sleep tonight, a soldier in the thick of battle, a loving father, an addict looking for the next fix, and so on.

Sentient beings of my mind are numberless; I vow to save them all.

BILL DEVALL

Suffering and Redemption

BILL DEVALL was a student of my dharma sister Maylie Scott. After she died, I gave lay ordination to Bill, with the name Keishin—Joyous Forest. Bill was tall, lanky, and cantankerous. For much of his distinguished scholarly career as a professor of sociology at Humboldt State University in Arcata, California, Bill deepened and extended the deep ecology work of Norwegian philosopher Arne Næss. More than a scholar, Bill was an activist, taking part in the 1990 Redwood Summer, which led to the consolidation of state and federal lands into Redwood National and State Parks in 1994.

Bill was always brightly alive, even at his most acerbic. He suffered from a range of chronic illnesses. One could see his pain simply in the way he held his body. On a family car trip to Oregon, we stopped to spend an evening with Bill and other Zen friends in Arcata. We had dinner and lively conversation at a Chinese buffet in a local mall. As we walked across the parking lot in a misting rain, Bill stopped me and asked bluntly, "Is suffering redemptive?" My immediate response was, "No." Bill snorted and walked away.

Why does this moment stay with me? Even today I think about his question. At this point, I can explain why I said no, but I will spare you the argument. Whether or not my thinking holds up, I know I answered Bill's question incorrectly. He was asking me to see him whole. The single word *no* shut the door between us. An opportunity missed. I wish we could play this over.

Bill Devall died in June 2009, at the age of seventy. I do not know if he answered his own question. From my perspective, he was a great soul, a wise man. But that is not always sustenance for a suffering person. At his memorial I read these words, which I had written on his *rakusu* at the time of lay ordination.

> Let go of emptiness and come back to the brambly forest.
> Riding backwards on the ox, drunken and singing,
> Who could dislike the misty rain pattering on your bam-
>   boo raincoat and hat?
> In empty space, you cannot stick a needle.

HONGZHI

B. R. AMBEDKAR

Liberty, Equality, Fraternity

I MAKE AN EXCEPTION to turning words that I heard myself to include the words and example of Dr. Bhimrao Ramji Ambedkar (1891–1956), liberator of India's "untouchables" and the founder of a contemporary movement of Indian Buddhism rooted in the oppressed classes, sometimes called Navayana Buddhism, the "new vehicle."

I read about Dr. Ambedkar when I was working at Parallax Press in 1989. Nagabodhi Terry Pilchik had just published a book with Parallax titled *Jai Bhim!: Dispatches from a Peaceful Revolution*, an account of his experiences among India's Ambedkarite Buddhist movement. On reading this I was sure that I wanted to see these remarkable communities for myself. In the meantime, I continued to read the work of Dr. Ambedkar, including his classic *Buddha and His Dhamma*. He was a polymath, with two doctorates—from Columbia University and London School of Economics. After his schooling, he was called to the bar at Gray's Inn in England in order to practice law. In 1947, he was invited to be the first law minister of a newly independent India, and in that position, he is seen as architect of the Indian Constitution.

It took me twenty years to make the right connections with the Ambedkarite Buddhist movement, but I did eventually travel to India, and have been working with Ambedkarites since 2009. These are treasured relationships. I am witness to a live expression of dharma that should be better known in the Buddhist world. I'm grateful, too, for opportunities to teach about the social application of Buddhism as I have experienced it in the United States and elsewhere in Asia.

At last I arrive at the turning words. In 1936, Dr. Ambedkar drafted a speech that rings in my ears like Dr. Martin Luther King Jr.'s "Letter from a Birmingham Jail." Invited to address an anticaste Hindu reformist group, which subsequently refused to let him speak, he wrote "Annihilation of Caste," which included these words: "If you ask me, my ideal would be a society based on Liberty, Equality, and Fraternity." He explained:

> It was, indeed, a way of life, which recognizes liberty, equality, and fraternity as the principles of life and which cannot be divorced from each other: Liberty cannot be divorced from equality; equality cannot be divorced from liberty. Nor can liberty and equality be divorced from fraternity. Without equality, liberty would produce the supremacy of the few over the many. Equality without liberty would kill individual initiative. Without fraternity, liberty and equality could not become a natural course of things.[12]

Thirteen years later, as law minister, he enshrined these principles in the Preamble to the Indian Constitution:

WE, THE PEOPLE OF INDIA, having solemnly resolved to constitute India into a *Sovereign Socialist Secular Democratic Republic* and to secure to all its citizens:

JUSTICE, social, economic and political;

LIBERTY of thought, expression, belief, faith and worship;

EQUALITY of status and of opportunity; and to promote among them all

FRATERNITY assuring the dignity of the individual and the unity and integrity of the Nation; *in our constituent assembly* this twenty-sixth day of November, 1949, do hereby adopt, enact, and give to *THIS CONSTITUTION.*

Like the US Constitution, this preamble and the Indian Constitution proper are high-minded documents whose full enactment we have yet to see. Still, for me, these are turning words.

HIS HOLINESS
THE DALAI LAMA

Snapshots from Hamburg

I HAD BRIEFLY ENCOUNTERED His Holiness the Dalai Lama twice before in public settings. In each case His Holiness went down a reception line, taking each person's hand, bowing his head while he looked in our eyes. This was a practice for him, acknowledging each being.

In August 2011 I took part in an International Conference on Mindfulness sponsored by the University of Hamburg in Germany. There were four days of presentations and panels, largely by European academics who were studying both practical and theoretical aspects of contemporary mindfulness—*Achtsamkeit*. Professor Michael Zimmermann, one of the key organizers, knew me from discussions we had had about engaged Buddhism while he was teaching at Stanford. I was honored to be invited, and this turned out to be the first of several fruitful visits to new friends in northern Germany.

The conference concluded with a public lecture and interview with His Holiness the Dalai Lama. Once again I was struck by his practice of personal connection. Coming out from backstage while the presenters were gathered to receive him, His Holiness walked up to each of us. I was wearing black travel robes and a *rakusu*, a small bib-like robe. His Holiness took my hand and said, "Oh . . . Zen Master." I quietly responded, "No . . . Zen Mister."

I was surprised to be seated directly next to His Holiness, just two feet or so from him. The striking thing is that I felt quite comfortable, not at all nervous. There was no buzz of holiness. Noticing that sense of normality, or ordinariness, I wondered how this might be the case. I've come to think that this is an essential part of the Dalai Lama's gift—to accept people and to put them at ease. Which, of course, makes things easier for him.

Before writing this reflection, I reviewed the video from his lecture and the interview. Aside from the essential wisdom of his words and responses, I was most impressed by his composure—the feeling that here was a man at home in his own body and mind.

There was a moment toward the end that got my attention. Michael was bringing the event to a graceful end after about two hours onstage. But one presenter wanted to make a last pronouncement. While this presenter spoke, His Holiness, still seated, put his feet on the floor, leaned over, and tied his shoes one at a time, his attention on the laces, not looking at the speaker. I thought, "Oh, he's human . . . he's done."

The conference ended the following morning. When we finished breakfast at the hotel, the entire hotel staff lined up to say goodbye to His Holiness and his retinue. Once again, he went down that line, smiling and shaking each person's hand. With a last wave, he departed.

JOAN JIKO HALIFAX

Zazen Instruction

I'VE BEEN TEACHING with Roshi Joan in the Upaya Chaplaincy Program since 2011, going to Santa Fe, New Mexico, twice a year to meet with the remarkable and dedicated student chaplains as they blossom in their two years of training. Joan Halifax is a brilliant light—a fearless intelligence, a heart open to the world, with a great gift for drawing bright lights around her.

The scope of her teaching is very wide, but two points of her zazen instruction stick in my mind. The first instruction I have taken to heart is to begin each period of zazen with the cultivation of *bodhicitta*—buddha-mind, or the thought of enlightenment. Bodhicitta takes many forms, but here it relates to the bodhisattva vow to attain enlightenment, motivated by compassion for all living beings.

While the teaching of bodhicitta was not new to me, this way of linking zazen and bodhisattva activity was fresh. It was not emphasized in the zazen instructions I had previously heard. So I thought for a while, then I tried it myself. I silently recite a verse to myself three times at the start of zazen: "May I be awake that others may awaken." I drop these words lightly into the pool of consciousness, then move on to an open, receptive awareness. I've now been doing this for years at the start of each zazen period.

The practice of zazen needs a physical foundation. It is a mind-body practice built on our stable, upright posture. Countless words of instruction have been offered to Zen students over the last thousand years. Roshi Joan says, "Strong back, soft front." This is the meeting place of wisdom and compassion. The strength of steel and the subtle power of receptivity. A perfect description of zazen.

In *Being with Dying*, Roshi Joan says,

All too often our so-called strength comes from fear not love; instead of having a strong back, many of us have a defended front shielding a weak spine. In other words, we walk around brittle and defensive, trying to conceal our lack of confidence. If we strengthen our backs, metaphorically speaking, and develop a spine that's flexible but sturdy, then we can risk having a front that's soft and open, representing choiceless compassion. The place in your body where these two meet—strong back and soft front—is the brave, tender ground in which to root our caring deeply.

How can we give and accept care with strong-back, soft-front compassion, moving past fear into a place of genuine tenderness? I believe it comes about when we can be truly transparent, seeing the world clearly—and letting the world see into us.[13]

KAREN DECOTIS

Do You Want to Be Right?

KAREN DECOTIS, whose dharma name is Sekishun Kanshi, is teacher at the Bozeman Zen Group in beautiful Montana. She is an old friend, a former resident at Berkeley Zen Center, who received dharma transmission from Sojun Roshi in the autumn of 2019.

There is a simple lesson I learned from Karen some years ago. Very simple. Ask yourself, "Do you want to be right, or do you want to be in connection?"

PAMELA AYO YETUNDE

Bible Study

PAMELA AYO YETUNDE is a force of nature—brilliant, articulate, and challenging. I met her in the Upaya Chaplaincy Training Program where she came in as a faculty member, given her experience and credentials in pastoral counseling. She wanted to refresh her spiritual formation as a chaplain, so while teaching she also enrolled as a student. In the few years since, she has emerged as a leading voice, coeditor of *Black and Buddhist: What Buddhism Can Teach Us about Race, Resilience, Transformation, and Freedom*, and cofounder of Center of the Heart.

In fall 2020, Ayo was keynote speaker at the Soto Zen Buddhist Association's online conference. In the course of her presentation on race, diversity, and Zen, Ayo was pointing out how little many of us in Zen communities knew about how Christianity is expressed in Black churches here in our own neighborhoods. She suggested that the easiest way to find out was to go to Bible study sessions at one of these churches. Digging around online, I found this transcription of what she actually said in her SZBA keynote:

> Here's what I think you could do, which I think would be awesome and would be wonderful for spiritual development, community development, and solidarity building. That is to commit in the year 2021 to attending, at least monthly, a Bible study or a church service at a Black church oriented around Black liberation. When you go there, tell them why you're there, listen, don't take up a lot of space, and attend in your Zen attire. This way you will understand what it takes to work with difference and to be perceived as strange, as we Black people are perceived oftentimes. But more importantly, to be immersed in Black Christian liberatory culture will go a long way toward solidarity between our groups.[14]

I thought about this. There is an African American evangelical church two blocks from Berkeley Zen Center that I passed on morning walks in the neighborhood. I had met the pastor a few years ago and meant to circle back, though it didn't happen. Now the pandemic was upon us, but I searched and found that this church, the Church by the Side of the Road, had online Bible study every Wednesday at noon.

I showed up one Wednesday online and was welcomed into their circle. This was a group of eight or ten African American Christians, roughly my age. I think they wondered how I had gotten there and why. But they were warm and inclusive. I had some private exchanges with the minister who led the group, so I could be transparent about my religious background and practice. Really, our congregations were only two blocks away from each other. The Bible study group did close reading and discussion of New and Old Testament texts. I did my best to set aside my Buddhist perspectives. The odd thing was that my Jewish education and ethnic background seemed to resonate more strongly with them than my Buddhist identity. So I was surprised to find myself inescapably Jewish.

Ayo's encouragement had moved me beyond my imagined comfort zone into a new territory of relationship that led across religious and racial lines. Just to see how clear these lines were within my mind and conditioning, I needed the simple push that Ayo gave us. Now, I bow in gratitude.

TETSUDO ROSS BLUM

The Spirit of Repetition

SOMETIMES A TURNING WORD is a joke, or a joke is a turning word.

On Tuesday evenings at Berkeley Zen Center, the residents gather for dinner and a meeting, where we have personal check-ins and go over any issues that may have come up recently. I've been going to these meetings for more than thirty-five years. Along with daily zazen, this is part of the fabric of practice that weaves us together as community. Also, we get to enjoy the flavors of each other's cooking week to week. My dharma brother Ross Blum has been attending almost as long as I have.

At the end of each meeting, the evening's cook opens one of Suzuki Roshi's books at random and reads a short passage aloud. On a recent night, the cook was Sojun Roshi's wife, Liz Horowitz, who has always been part of these meetings.

She picked up a copy of *Zen Mind, Beginner's Mind*, flipped through the pages, and read out the chapter heading "The Spirit of Repetition."

Immediately Ross said, "Not that again . . ."

WE'RE STILL SITTING
SILENTLY...

AT MIDNIGHT on February 9, 1999, Jaturun Siripongs was executed by lethal injection at San Quentin State Prison in California. He had been convicted of robbery and double murder at a small store in Garden Grove, California, where he had previously worked. "Jay" Siripongs was a Thai national, who had briefly been a Theravada monk in Thailand. While legal efforts were underway until the last moment, California governor Gray Davis rejected the defense's plea for clemency, which had been joined by two jurors, a former San Quentin warden, the government of Thailand, and the husband of one of Siripongs's victims.

In his final week, Jay was visited by Ajahn Pasanno, coabbot of Abhayagiri Monastery in Mendocino County. Bhante Pasanno wrote about that final evening:

We spent the whole evening meditating, chanting, and talking Dhamma. So in the last hour Jay was very peaceful and able to establish his mind firmly on his meditation object. Toward the end, we took the time to do a ceremony of sharing merit and offering blessings, even to the guards.

At the prison entrance a cold rain was falling. There were about two hundred people gathered in front of the tall steel gates. These were mostly death penalty opponents, peppered with a few vocal death penalty advocates. Huddled on blue tarps where the rain pooled, about seventy-five meditators from several Buddhist traditions sat in the midst of the whole catastrophe. This action was organized by Buddhist Peace Fellowship and was the first organized Buddhist execution vigil, a tradition that continued at each of the seven subsequent executions at San Quentin until 2006, when execution protocols were legally challenged and a moratorium was imposed.

I sat on my black cushion in the rain for hours, until we received notice of Siripongs's death. My robes were soaked through and I was actually shaking with the cold and damp. On the other side of the iron gates, about fifteen or twenty California Highway Patrolmen in helmets and riot gear stood in the same downpour, rotating out every hour.

There was radio and television coverage, with several reporters set up on the flat roof of the visitor's gatehouse to the east of the main gate. One reporter stood there with his microphone while his cameraman panned from him to our sodden meditators. In a stage whisper, I heard him say, "They're sitting silently." After about a minute—which is a lot of dead air on radio or television—he said, "They're still sitting silently . . ."

At the heart of Zen, this is what we do. We sit upright—in rain and cold, in loss and uncertainty, in sorrow and joy. Sitting silently, then arising to offer an appropriate response.

ACKNOWLEDGMENTS

I begin by bowing deeply to my root teacher, Sojun Mel Weitsman Roshi, for thirty-eight years of scrutiny, training, and the deepest compassion. Then I offer the great circle of an all-inclusive bow to the teachers evoked in these pages and the countless beings, known and unknown, who continue to reveal the path.

Susan Moon, old friend and fellow traveler, graced *Turning Words* with a wonderful foreword. Matt Zepelin brought this book into the Shambhala fold and helped shape it. I am deeply grateful to have worked with him and then with Liz Shaw, who carried the project to completion after Matt and his wife Kelly became parents to Lily Rae. Editors Gretchen Gordon and Peter Schumacher, who precisely tended to myriad small but necessary details, kept me on track. And a bow to Emily Coughlin, the editor with whom I was initially partnered until the birth of her daughter, Mabel. Thanks as well to the great design team at Shambhala.

May our children inherit the dharma and step forward for the sake of all beings, sentient and insentient.

—HOZAN ALAN SENAUKE

AUGUST 2022

NOTES

1. "The Work That Reconnects," Joanna Macy (website), accessed May 17, 2022, https://www.joannamacy.net/work.
2. Joanna Macy, "Joanna Macy on How to Prepare Internally for WHATEVER Comes Next," Films for Action (website), May 27, 2016, https://www.filmsforaction.org/articles/joanna-macy -on-how-to-prepare-internally-for-whatever-comes-next/.
3. Kazuaki Tanahashi, ed., *Moon in a Dewdrop: Writings by Zen Master Dogen* (Berkeley, CA: Northpoint Press, 1985), 71.
4. Shunryu Suzuki, *Zen Mind, Beginner's Mind: Informal Talks on Zen Meditation and Practice* (New York: Weatherhill, 1986), 116.
5. Quoted in Charles S. Prebish and Kenneth K. Tanaka, eds., *The Faces of Buddhism in America* (Berkeley: University of California Press, 1998), 68–69.
6. Arnie Kotler, preface to *Being Peace* (Berkeley, CA: Parallax Press, 1987), vii.
7. Thich Nhat Hanh, "Mindfulness Must Be Engaged," in *Peace Is Every Step* (Berkeley, CA: Parallax Press, 1991), 91.
8. Thich Nhat Hanh, *Peace Is Every Step*, 91.
9. Thich Nhat Hanh, "We Are the Beaters; We Are the Beaten," *Los Angeles Times*, April 15, 1991. https://www.latimes.com/ archives/la-xpm-1991-04-15-me-32-story.html/.
10. Robert Aitken, *The Gateless Barrier* (San Francisco: North Point Press, 1990), 7.
11. Maha Ghosananda, *Step by Step* (Berkeley, CA: Parallax Press, 1992), 39.

12. B. R. Ambedkar, "Annihilation of Caste with a Reply to Mahatma Gandhi," Section XIV, Dr. Babasaheb Ambedkar & His People (website), accessed May 17, 2022, http://www.ambedkar.org/ambcd/02.Annihilation%20of%20Caste.htm.

13. Joan Jiko Halifax, *Being with Dying* (Boston: Shambhala Publications, 2008), 17.

14. Used by permission of Pamela Ayo Yetunde.

RESOURCES

SELECTED BIBLIOGRAPHY

Aitken, Robert, trans.. *The Gateless Barrier: The Wu-Men Kuan (Mumonkan)*. San Francisco: North Point Press, 1991.
———. *The Mind of Clover: Essays in Zen Buddhist Ethics*. San Francisco: North Point Press, 1984.
———. *Taking the Path of Zen*. San Francisco: North Point Press, 1982.
Ambedkar, B. R. *The Buddha and His Dhamma*. New Delhi: Oxford University Press, 2011.
———. *The Essential Writings of B. R. Ambedkar*. New Delhi: Oxford University Press, 2002.
Anderson, Reb. *Being Upright: Zen Meditation and Bodhisattva Precepts*. Berkeley, CA: Rodmell Press, 2000.
———. *Entering the Mind of Buddha: Zen and the Six Heroic Practices of Bodhisattvas*. Boulder, CO: Shambhala Publications, 2019.
———. *The Third Turning of the Wheel: Wisdom of the Samdhinirmocana Sutra*. Berkeley, CA: Rodmell Press, 2012.
Chadwick, David. *Crooked Cucumber: The Life and Teaching of Shunryu Suzuki*. New York: Broadway Books, 1999.
———. *Thank You and OK! An American Zen Failure in Japan*. Boston: Shambhala Publications, 2007.
Dalai Lama, His Holiness the Fourteenth (Tenzin Gyatso), with Howard C. Cutler. *The Art of Happiness: A Handbook for Living*. 10th ann. ed. New York: Riverhead Books, 2009.

———. *Ethics for a New Millennium*. New York: Riverhead Books, 2001.

———. *Healing Anger: The Power of Patience from a Buddhist Perspective*. Ithaca, NY: Snow Lion Publications, 1997.

Foster, Nelson, and Jack Shoemaker, eds. *The Roaring Stream: A New Zen Reader*. Hopewell, NJ: Ecco Press, 1997.

Ghosananda, Maha. *Step by Step*. Berkeley, CA: Parallax Press, 1992.

Glassman, Bernie. *Bearing Witness: A Zen Master's Lessons in Making Peace*. New York: Harmony, 1998.

———. *Infinite Circle: Teachings in Zen*. Boston: Shambhala Publications, 2002.

Glassman, Bernie, and Rick Fields. *Instructions to the Cook: A Zen Master's Lessons in Living a Life That Matters*. New York: Bell Tower, 1996.

Halifax, Joan. *Being with Dying: Cultivating Compassion and Fearlessness in the Presence of Death*. Boston: Shambhala Publications, 2008.

———. *Standing at the Edge: Finding Freedom Where Fear and Courage Meet*. New York: Flatiron Books, 2018.

Harada, Shodo. *Moon by the Window: The Calligraphy and Zen Insights of Shodo Harada*. Wisdom, 2011.

———. *Not One Single Thing: Commentary on the Platform Sutra*. Somerville, MA: Wisdom Publications, 2018.

———. *The Path to Bodhidharma: The Teachings of Shodo Harada Roshi*. Boston: Tuttle, 2000.

Huineng, Dajian. *The Platform Sutra: The Zen Teaching of Hui-neng*. Translated by Red Pine. Berkeley, CA: Counterpoint, 2008.

Katagiri, Dainin. *Each Moment Is the Universe: Zen and the Way of Being Time*. Boston: Shambhala Publications, 2008.

———. *Returning to Silence: Zen Practice in Everyday Life*. Boston: Shambhala Publications, 1988.

———. *You Have to Say Something: Manifesting Zen Insight*. Boston: Shambhala Publications, 1988.

Macy, Joanna. *Mutual Causality in Buddhism and General Systems Theory: The Dharma of Natural Systems*. Albany: State University of New York Press, 1991.

———. *World as Lover, World as Self: Courage for Global Justice and Ecological Renewal*. Berkeley, CA: Parallax Press, 2007.

Macy, Joanna, and Chris Johnstone. *Active Hope: How to Face the Mess We're In without Going Crazy*. Novato, CA: New World Library, 2012.

Masters, Jarvis Jay. *Finding Freedom: How Death Row Broke and Opened My Heart*. Boulder, CO: Shambhala Publications, 2020.

———. *That Bird Has My Wings: The Autobiography of an Innocent Man on Death Row*. New York: HarperOne, 2010.

Nhat Hanh, Thich. *Being Peace*. Berkeley, CA: Parallax Press, 1987.

———. *The Heart of the Buddha's Teaching: Transforming Suffering into Peace, Joy, and Liberation*. New York: Broadway Books, 2015.

———. *The Miracle of Mindfulness: An Introduction to the Practice of Meditation*. Boston: Beacon Press, 1996.

———. *Peace Is Every Step: The Path of Mindfulness in Everyday Life*. Berkeley, CA: Parallax Press, 1992.

———. "We Are the Beaters; We Are the Beaten." *Los Angeles Times*. April 15, 1991. https://www.latimes.com/archives/la-xpm-1991-04-15-me-32-story.html.

Otogawa, Kobun Chino. *Embracing Mind: The Zen Talks of Kobun Chino Otogawa*. Edited by Judy Cosgrove and Shinbo Joseph Hall. Los Gatos, CA: Jikoji Zen Center, 2016.

Pistono, Matteo. *Roar: Sulak Sivaraksa and the Path of Socially Engaged Buddhism*. Berkeley, CA: North Atlantic Books, 2019.

Sangharakshita. *Ambedkar and Buddhism*. New Delhi: Motilal Banarsidass, 2006.

Senauke, Hozan Alan. *The Bodhisattva's Embrace: Dispatches from Engaged Buddhism's Front Lines*. Berkeley, CA: Clear View, 2010.

———. *Everything Is Broken: Songs about Things as They Are* (CD). Berkeley, CA: Clear View 2012.

———. *Heirs to Ambedkar: The Rebirth of Engaged Buddhism in India.* Berkeley, CA: Clear View, 2014.

———. *Words of My Perfect Teacher.* Berkeley, CA: Clear View, 2019.

Sheff, David. *The Buddhist on Death Row: How One Man Found Light in the Darkest Place.* New York: Simon & Schuster, 2020.

Sheng Yen. *Faith in Mind: A Commentary on Seng Ts'an's Classic.* Boston: Shambhala Publications, 2008.

———. *Hoofprint of the Ox: Principles of the Chan Buddhist Path as Taught by a Modern Chinese Master.* Oxford: Oxford University Press, 2002.

———. *The Method of No-Method: The Chan Practice of Silent Illumination.* Boston: Shambhala Publications, 2008.

Sivaraksa, Sulak. *Seeds of Peace: A Buddhist Vision for Renewing Society.* Berkeley, CA: Parallax Press, 1992.

———. *Wisdom of Sustainability: Buddhist Economics for the 21st Century.* Kihei, HI: Koa Books, 2016.

Trungpa, Chögyam. *Cutting Through Spiritual Materialism.* Boulder, CO: Shambhala Publications, 1973.

———. *Meditation in Action.* Boulder, CO: Shambhala Publications, 1969.

———. *The Myth of Freedom and the Way of Meditation.* Boulder, CO: Shambhala Publications, 1976.

Yetunde, Pamela Ayo, and Cheryl Giles, eds. *Black and Buddhist: What Buddhism Can Teach Us about Race, Resilience, Transformation, and Freedom.* Boulder, CO: Shambhala Publications, 2020.

WEBSITES AND LINKS

Tenshin Reb Anderson: https://rebanderson.org
David Chadwick: www.cuke.com
Joan Jiko Halifax: www.upaya.org

Joanna Macy: www.joannamacy.net
Jarvis Jay Masters: www.freejarvis.org
Thich Nhat Hanh: https://plumvillage.org
Santikaro: www.kevalaretreat.org
Hozan Alan Senauke: http://clearviewproject.org
Sojun Mel Weitsman: https://berkeleyzencenter.org
Pamela Ayo Yetunde: www.centeroftheheart.org

PHOTO CREDITS

All photos used by permission of photographer or copyright holder.

pages 52, 54 Chitose and Hoitsu Suzuki—Photo © Hozan Alan Senauke, Hoitsu and Chitose Suzuki San Francisco, 2010.

page 58 Laurie Senauke—Photo © Hozan Alan Senauke, Laurie Senauke, Berkeley Zen Center, 2019.

page 60 Ven. Sheng Yen—Photo © courtesy of Dharma Drum Mountain Cultural and Educational Foundation.

page 63 Thich Nhat Hanh—Photo © by Gaetano Kazuo Maida, TNH at Berkeley Community Theater, 1993.

page 67 Santikaro—Photo © Hozan Alan Senauke, Santikaro, Ithaca, NY, 1999.

page 70 Sulak Sivaraksa—Photo © Hozan Alan Senauke, Sulak Sivaraksa, San Francisco, 2009.

page 73 Robert Aitken—Photo © Hozan Alan Senauke, Robert Aitken, Hawaii, 2001.

page 77 Maha Ghosananda—Photo © Hozan Alan Senauke, Maha Ghosananda, Spirit Rock, CA, 2000.

page 82 Bernie Tetsugen Glassman—Photo © Hozan Alan Senauke, Bernie Glassman, Berkeley Zen Center, 2002.

page 84 Nelson Foster—Photo © Masako Cordray, "Nelson Foster, Waipi'o," 2017.

page 86 Joseph Goldstein— Photo © Courtesy of Insight Meditation Society.

page 89 Jarvis Masters—Photo courtesy of Hozan Alan Senauke, Jarvis Jay Masters, San Quentin State Prison, CA, 2018.

page 93 Shodo Harada—Photo © Hozan Alan Senauke, Shodo Harada, calligraphy demonstration, LACMA, Los Angeles, 2002.

page 95 Seisho Maylie Scott—Photo © Hozan Alan Senauke, Maylie Scott, Arcata Zen Center, 1999.

page 97 Bhante Suhita Dharma—Photo © Hozan Alan Senauke, Bhante Suhita Dharma, outside Buddhist Peace Fellowship office, Oakland, CA, 2006.

page 99 Dajian Huineng—Painting, source unknown.

page 101 Bill Devall—Photo © Hozan Alan Senauke, Bill Devall, Arcata Zen Center, 2007.

page 104 B. R. Ambedkar—Photo © Hozan Alan Senauke, photographic plaque of Dr. Ambedkar, Nagpur, India, 2010.

page 107 His Holiness the Dalai Lama—Photo © by Gaetano Kazuo Maida, Tenzin Gyatso, the Fourteenth Dalai Lama, in Santa Barbara, 1990.

page 110 Joan Jiko Halifax—Photo © Hozan Alan Senauke, Joan Jiko Halifax, Spirit Rock, CA, 2000.

page 111 Karen DeCotis—Photo © Hozan Alan Senauke, Karen DeCotis, Berkeley Zen Center, 2019.

page 114 Pamela Ayo Yetunde—Photo © Miriam Phields, Pamela Ayo Yetunde, 2017.

page 116 Tetsudo Ross Blum—Photo © Hozan Alan Senauke, Tetsudo Ross Blum, Berkeley, CA, 2022.

page 132 Hozan Alan Senauke (author photo)—Photo © Cira Crowell, "Portrait of Hozan at Wayring Temple, Santa Fe," 2016.

ABOUT THE AUTHOR

HOZAN ALAN SENAUKE is a Soto Zen Buddhist priest, abbot of Berkeley Zen Center in California. After years with Buddhist Peace Fellowship and the International Network of Engaged Buddhists, Hozan founded Clear View Project, offering Buddhist-based resources for social change in Asia and the United States. He is past president of the Soto Zen Buddhist Association.

Hozan often writes about engaged Buddhism, with books available from Amazon.com and from www.clearviewproj ect.org. He is also a father, activist, student, and performer of American traditional music with numerous albums and recordings.